# WRIT LEVISION

# *Writing for Radio and Television*

By
ROY LOMAX

Roy Lomax
WRITING FOR RADIO AND TELEVISION

First Published 1982

ISBN 0 906486 03 3

Writing School Guides
Published in Great Britain by
CLAREFEN LIMITED
18–20 High Road, Wood Green,
London N22 6BX

Set printed and bound in Great Britain
by Billing and Sons Limited,
Guildford, London, Oxford, Worcester.

# Contents

# Introduction

The infant television made its entry into our lives shortly after the end of World War II. Since then it has developed into a form of communication and entertainment which towers above everything else.

In the earliest years of its development, necessary as he was, the TV scriptwriter received little reward and even less credit for his efforts. The few dramatic presentations at the beginning were mainly drawn from past stage successes and, to some extent, from programmes first heard on radio. Even the early comedians supplied their own club or stage routines and gags.

Those were the days of live transmissions, complete with scenery which was often not much better than that built for amateur theatricals in a village hall. There were doors which jammed at a crucial moment, matches which refused to light, boom microphones which could be seen hovering over the heads of the actors and studio lights which fused at the worst possible time. There was also, more often than not, the stage-hand who wandered, unaware, in front of the camera, or suddenly looked in on us through a window when we were supposed to be up in an apartment on the 52nd floor.

It was a period of learning for actors, producers, technicians and scriptwriters alike, and a time when, Riley's Law was almost a way of life – Whatever can go wrong, *will* go wrong!

By present day standards, the early TV productions seem to be quite amateurish. But what the people who made them lacked in experience with the new medium, they compensated for with enthusiasm and hard sweat. And so this infant grew – as the comedian Arthur Askey has it – right before your very eyes!

From whence did these early scriptwriters come? You can name any area that you wish, and you are almost certain to be right. But the best of them certainly had some experience in writing for radio. It would be unfair to both these media to claim that one or the other is the inferior member of a pair of twins. But it would be true to say that TV served a short apprenticeship to radio in order to learn the basic skills. So the would-be TV scriptwriter should look on radio as his first and most important area of study. Here he should concentrate on gaining the mastery of the art of story-telling, entertaining and communicating his ideas in the most basic form, preparing for the time when he can move over to TV, where he will find that the skills he now requires are not so much the techniques of *expanding* on his methods of presentation but of *refining* and *reducing* them.

This becomes more than apparent when we consider how a 'big' story is best told on radio or on TV: a story which is 'big' in every respect in action, in location and in size of cast.

Let us say that you have chosen to write a play which uses Messrs. Stanley and Livingstone as the principal players. You decide to build your drama through scenes enacted in America, in London, at Southampton Docks, on board an ocean-going ship, at an African port swarming with people, on a riverboat and in dugout canoes. You want your characters to struggle through animal-infested steaming jungles, splash through eerie swamps and scale a cliff alongside a thundering waterfall. There will certainly be a moment when you consider using a hundred or so natives either as porters or unfriendly types who will attack your brave heroes or, perhaps, hold their own special brand of whoopie party to celebrate something or other.

With a cast of six actors and some special effect records; with some slick skulduggery on the part of a sound engineer, and with some pre-recording and mixing – radio can present your play just as well as it can a kitchen-sink story.

But apart from a book, the only other medium which could come anywhere close to telling your story on such a grand scale would be the cinema film. And to achieve the same result as your economical radio play which is rehearsed and recorded in one working day, the film company would need to spend millions of pounds and possibly take a year in production.

Of course, you can tell the same basic story through the television screen. But your presentation would need to be *refined* and *reduced*. A great deal would need to be played in specially built studio sets. Perhaps some scenes could be filmed inside areas such as an old London hotel, or the study of a grand old stately house. Your Southampton Docks of yesteryear and the spray-soaked deck of a ship are no more available to you than the hundred or so natives, the waterfall, the crocodiles and the swamps. Possibly, and only possibly, the TV company would consider using a piece of ground not too distant from their home base which would be dressed with tropical plants to give it some semblance of being a jungle. But if your play is one of those churned out on a budget – you could well find that you must settle for even less than that.

It has been said before that radio has the best scenery in the world. You can extend that to include the best costumes, the best props and the most daring of dramatic action. Crowd scenes may be as large as you care to make them. Your hero may manfully struggle with six giant wild dogs, dive headlong from the Golden Gate Bridge, and drive his Lagonda at ninety miles an hour through a frontier barrier guarded by a dozen machine carbines and a minefield. All this is readily available to you on radio.

Very few radio plays are, in fact, as 'big' as the one which we have just been discussing. Most of them are quieter and of a more intimate nature. But even here radio has its own advantages over televison.

Let us consider one of these quieter and more intimate stories. Herbert Jones and his wife Molly are the proprietors of a small general store in a quiet English village, where they have lived, worked and raised a family during the past thirty five years. They have sold the shop and are moving away tomorrow. Your story is to quietly investigate their innermost feelings concerning this their last day. Will they be glad to be rid of the place, with all of its dull familiarity and lack of excitement? Or, over the years has it become so much part of themselves that it is, in fact, a kind of family album rich with sweet memories of those happy years? You can shape this plot in many, many ways, but you are more or less confined to playing the action in the shop, the back room, the living quarters above, and perhaps the street outside.

A television version of this same play would probably seem to be claustrophobic. Any coming and going of non-participating customers (called moving scenery) would have to be so minimal as to give the impression to the viewer that this business was about to fold up owing to lack of trade – and this can often be observed in those 'soap-opera' TV serials which consistently use pub bars, hotel receptions, restaurants and the like.

With a radio version, the shop background could be as quiet or as busy as the writer thought necessary. And the sound microphone has the unique ability of seeming to carry its own location with it. When Herbert is serving a customer with bread and carrying on an important piece of dialogue for the plot, we can hear his wife faintly 'off-mike' in some activity of her own. Is she serving at another counter? Or standing at the doorway? Up a step-ladder? Or even in the room at the back with the door open? It doesn't much matter where she is. We know that she is at a distance from her husband, and our own minds will fill in all of the imaginary scenic detail that is necessary for us to believe that we are in the ideal shop for this story.

When once George Bernard Shaw was asked to give his opinion on the subject of marriage, he said – "It provides the maximum of temptation with the maximum of opportunity."

For the scriptwriter, the same statement could as well be said of radio. It truly is an Alice-in-Wonderland world where anything is possible, where tales of great age and fury may be told; where we may inspect the microbe in all its detail, and where the simple stories of ordinary people may be invested with everything from rich humour to the deepest of tragedy.

It is in the medium of radio where all the essential tricks of the scriptwriting trade are best learned, so we shall begin this book right there. Most radio scriptwriters eventually progress to writing for the box. Very, very few writers who start by writing for television are able to do as well on radio.

# I

# *Writing for Radio*

# Chapter One

## THE MACHINERY OF RADIO

*Submitting the script*

The whole purpose of writing a radio play should be to have it accepted, broadcast and paid for. The aspiring writer should never automatically assume that he possesses some God-given right which will ensure that his particular script will be accepted. Even the most experienced scriptwriter will have his occasional rejection. That is the bad news. The good news is that the payments for acceptances are usually large enough for a certain amoung of wastage to be acceptable to the writer. The important trick is, not to have too much wastage.

Let us suppose that you have just written your first radio script. We shall say that it has a superb plot, is excellently written with brilliant dialogue and has taken years off your life in the writing. You submit it to a radio script department, and ten minutes or ten months after you have posted it, you find it sitting very solidly on your doormat with a polite note for having let them see it, but no thank you!

What is all this about? You did everything which you were supposed to do, including sending along a stamped addressed envelope – even signing your letter 'Your humble servant'.

Small wonder that you may go off your food and life in general for a few days and even consider going back to your more certain hobby of aiming for the top dividend of a football pool. If your manuscript is as good as we have supposed, then it could well be that you have only *submitted it at the wrong time*.

Perhaps your story is a Victorian thriller, a nice piece about murder, arsenic and a will, with plenty of London fog (which comes over very well on radio), cloppety-cloppety horse-drawn carriages and housemaids who put all their aitches in the wrong place. What you didn't know is that the radio company have three Victorian thrillers 'in the can' waiting for broadcasting. One has murder, another has cyanide, the other concerns a will. They all have London fog, cloppety-cloppety horses and creaking doors. A maid drops aitches in two of them, the other has a crook who doesn't use aitches at all.

What is even more depressing is that the script unit also has a few more scripts similar to yours which have been accepted and stockpiled for some future date.

What do you suppose your chances really are of getting an acceptance right at this moment? Surely, not too good. And what do you suppose your chances may be a year from now when the stockpile mainly consists of plays concerning modern mixed marriages? Cloppety-cloppety horses and radio fog may come as a blessed novelty then!

Medical doctors are very familiar with the fact that accidents and illnesses seem to appear in regularly occurring cycles. This is obviously understandable with epidemics such as influenza and impetigo. There are good reasons why there are tummy upsets just after Christmas and sunburns in the summer. What is not so understandable is that a doctor could have five different children brought to him in one week with a small button lodged up the nose. If you should happen to have your own personal small disaster, then you will probably find that many other people have experienced the same thing at the same time – which tends to cut down on the amount of sympathy that you may expect!

Perhaps then, we should not be so surprised that readers of manuscripts – for any of the media – find that a subject very often homes in on their desk in the form of half a hundred manuscripts, like a swarm of bees from the same hive.

It is also possible that the script department which you favoured with your first effort has simply accepted too many scripts and has consequently been told in no uncertain terms from above that no more may be taken until some later date. The person who reads your play may believe that it is the best thing he has ever seen, but he cannot be reasonably expected to press your case to the point of resigning on a matter of principle.

If you are now feeling that this submission of your first effort is going to be a complete waste of your time, then you may take heart from the fact that the two problems already mentioned can, to a large extent, be easily overcome.

There is nothing to prevent you from sending a preliminary letter of enquiry first to the script unit. You could say:

Dear Sir,

I have written a sixty-minute play which deals with a Victorian cloppety-cloppety horse who is searching for some cyanide in a London fog. He has a will of his own ... etc., etc.

Is this the kind of material which you are prepared to consider at the moment?

One way or another, you should receive a reply. Some companies will assure you that they will consider all work offered at any time. At least you will have checked that there is nothing to bar your way.

If you *are* advised to submit at a later date, then put your script safely to one side and get on with writing something else. The way to beat those stockpiles is to have one of your own!

We must also mention here that you should never destroy a script just because it appears to be unwanted at the moment. At some later time when you are well established and have good connections of your own, this script could possibly be brought out, dusted off and, perhaps with a rewrite, find a good home. Most successful writers had this experience with some of their early ugly ducklings.

So, your script is ready and you have satisfied yourself as far as you can that there is no good reason why it should not be put in the post.

Another piece of information which should be of use to you is that most script units (in any of the media) often do not have enough readers from time to time. When your work is received, it will usually be logged in a register, acknowledged to you, and then join the queue. Of course, a responsible reading unit will be hopefully looking for excellent material to buy. But you should always remember that great mounds of manuscripts awaiting consideration can begin to look quite formidable to those whose task it is to read them and it would only be natural for there to be the human impulse to reduce these piles by whatever legitimate means were available.

There may also be some kind of grading system in operation as a result of which the better scripts are moved into fresh piles for further consideration – and delay. The important lesson that you should learn right now is: once you have submitted your script – forget about it for the time being. Scripts rarely get lost and will usually surface out of the system in their own good time.

If you become unduly impatient and press for a prompt decision, then you may get the one that you do not want. Your script could be hauled out of its turn, given a hurried examination, and be returned to you with thanks. What is more – premature pestering by a writer brands him as an absolute amateur or, even worse, somebody who may be a pain in the neck to deal with. If you want to check on your submission, then do so gently and only if your better judgement assures you that the time is right.

We have assumed that you have not yet had anything accepted for radio. You don't know anyone in the organization, and nobody knows you. You have submitted your work stone cold and its fate is more or less in the lap of the gods. Most literary agents will not be interested in handling you at this stage as you are still very much an unknown quantity. You need to have faith in yourself and in your work, and must be prepared to negotiate this first hurdle very much on your own. Even if your work is of a high calibre, you may find that you need to submit more than one play before you have your first contract. Any plays which have 'bounced' you will, of course, keep safely for the reasons that we have mentioned before.

Later on in this book, we shall consider the proposition of 'milking an idea dry'. Sufficient for the moment to say that although you are putting the *radio* script to one side for a later submission, you may well be using the same plot for several other purposes.

To sum up, then: you have posted off the best radio play that you are capable of writing at the moment, and you are prepared to wait for as long as it takes for it to be considered. In fact, you are saying to yourself – "The longer they keep it – the better my chances." Having done this, then get your head down to writing something even better!

### *Your script is accepted*

To be more accurate, you will probably receive a letter from a producer who has taken an interest in your play which tells you that it has not been rejected. You may possibly get an invitation to call on him and discuss it. If you do, then make every effort to do so – even if you have to tell your boss that your third grandmother has died, and you must pawn the family jewels to raise the fare.

Whether you are writing for radio, for TV, for the bookshelf or the Press, you should take as many opportunities as you can to accept invitations from those who could buy your work. The keyword is *invitation*, which is not the same as you deciding that you should move into his office and take up more or less permanent residence.

This producer could make one of four proposals to you.

He could say that this present play is not one that he can accept, but he sees some promise in you as a writer. He could suggest that you try your hand at another story, and may even mention some areas of drama which would be particularly interesting to him. In any event, if you do your best and follow any advice that he gives you, then you should be able to make your first sale.

Or, he may tell you that he considers your play to be like the curate's egg, which is very good in parts. He may point out the weak points and ask you to submit a few pages showing how you would strengthen the piece. More often than not, you will find that you come away from the meeting with all the information that you need in order to satisfy him that he is justified in commissioning you to undertake a rewrite. Here, commissioning means being paid half the fee in advance.

The third possibility is that he will immediately commission you to rewrite the play. It is 'nearly there'. Perhaps it is a little too long, or needs building up in parts.

The fourth possibility is that he has decided to accept your play exactly as it is, but is interested in you telling him any ideas you may have about suitable actors or of any special background with which you may be particularly familiar.

### *Your words in action*

If your play is accepted by the BBC, then you will almost certainly have the invitation or opportunity to attend the studio for the recording. This is an experience that is not to be missed, for you will gain a first-hand knowledge of what really goes on in the studio which will give your writing of future scripts a new dimension and enable you to use all the technical resources to full advantage.

It will also add to your further listening pleasure, when you can say smugly to yourself: "Ah, yes – they've moved to the hard acoustic and Spotty is rustling the foil." With this personally observed material at your finger-tips, you can begin to write with some authority – and perhaps be difficult to live with!

Armed with your copy of the studio script which will have been sent to you by post, you present yourself at Broadcasting House at the appointed time and day and get yourself directed to the studio which is to be used for the production. This consists of two separate parts. The control room, and the main studio area.

The control room is the size of a rather largish office and has a large glass window looking down and into the studio area. The two parts of the studio are completely soundproofed from each other, but have their own communication link. Below the window is a long control panel. From here, every piece of electrical equipment in the whole suite may be operated singly or together. The remainder of the control room is equipped with several record turntables, three or so tape recorders and various other pieces of complex gadgetry.

The sound engineer sits at the control panel with the producer at his side. Behind the producer sits his secretary, complete with stop-watch, notebook and typewriter and telephone close to hand. If you, the author, are present – then this is where you will also sit. There will be two other people present in the control room. The assistant sound engineer will be tending to the tapes on which the programme is recorded and generally helping the sound engineer. There will also be the special effects assistant, who will be providing and mixing the music, storms, barking dogs and traffic from special discs and tapes.

There is one more member of the studio team, and that is the studio assistant – usually known as 'Spotty', from his or her responsibility for arranging spot microphones. This is the often hard-working individual who can be heard opening and closing doors, tramping in gravel, firing pistols, rattling cutlery and punching a hard bolster during a radio fight. In other words, all special effects which cannot be produced with the aid of the equipment within the control room.

The studio area is usually about the size of a small dance hall, with hard walls in some place and soft walls dressed with cork tiles or curtains in others. Thus a complete range of background acoustic can be provided for whatever your play demands. Here you will find various doors with knockers and bells, and mobile cupboards with as many entrances as a Chinese wardrobe. Stairs lead up to landings which go nowhere at all, and these stairs will be stone in part, and timber and carpeted in others.

There will be a large tank of water, complete with faucet and various home-made gadgets for creating many distinctive sounds of 'sploshing' – from Grannie doing the washing-up, to the sinking of the Titanic. There will be a large bed of gravel and stones, bundles of rustly materials and boxes of mysterious junk which, as the religionist tells us 'has its proper place in the noble order of existence.'

There will also be an area fitted with armchairs and coffee tables.

This is where discussions take place between the producer and the cast, and where the cast will sit whilst waiting their turns to perform at the microphone. This can be just a little disconcerting to the author on his first visit to the studio.

His hero and his villain may be locked in mortal combat over the fair lady at the microphone. There could be great effort and emotion, with sweat pouring from a number of brows and with Spotty punching seven colours of daylight out of the studio dummy. It takes considerable aplomb on the part of the author to watch this action for the first time, and to also see the 'fair lady' concerned comfortably sitting in the background with her feet up – oblivious to the activities of the contestants as she eats a cheese roll and checks her horoscope in a woman's magazine.

The author will probably be just as surprised when she comes to the microphone and wrings tears from his eyes – with the hero and villain only a few feet away swopping their holiday snaps.

What the author has to bear in mind is that just as he received his copy of the script before the day of recording, so did the studio crew and the cast. Everybody concerned has an understanding to a large degree of what is expected of them. If the author has written a particularly good piece, then he will find that he will receive proper professional appreciation. To expect a show of awe and overreverence for his work in the studio is expecting it from the wrong source – that should come from the radio audience. The very best results occur when all those participating are having fun. Yes, even when working on the most harrowing and dramatic of stories.

So, the author arrives at the studio armed with his copy of the script and is all prepared for a day or two of enjoyment. There is only one unbreakable rule which he should apply to himself. If there is any comment that he wishes to make concerning the script, the performance of the actors, or the technical activities of the studio staff – then he *should always make these to the producer* – preferably out of earshot of anyone else.

It is absolutely unforgiveable for the author to make direct comment on the work of any other professional involved in the production.

Of course, if anyone asks you a question, then you are free to answer as you please. Just be tactful. Nor do you have to sit there as silently as Spottie's long-suffering dummy. But the last thing that the producer wants is some know-all to upset the job in hand.

Having arrived, the producer will almost certainly introduce you to his secretary and the studio crew, and then have a few minutes chat with you. If the cast have all arrived, he will take you out into the studio and introduce you to them. You may take it for granted that actors will always receive a new writer extremely well. There will usually be an unspoken invitation to join their camaraderie which will soon have you feeling that you are 'one of the boys.' It is indeed a stupid author who gives the impression of being stand-offish for no good reason. Quite apart from the opportunity to enjoy new acquaintanceships, it is important for him to know and be known by as many people as possible in the industry if he wishes to find a place for himself in it.

You, the producer and his secretary – complete with stopwatch and notebook – will now sit down with the cast for the initial read-through of the script. Meantime, the studio crew will be setting up microphones, checking levels and acoustics and perhaps beginning to prerecord some of the special effects.

The read-through should be considered as an opportunity for breaking the ice, although its main function is to enable the producer's secretary to approximately time every scene and make a rough estimate of the overall length. It is not at all unusual here for the actors to get as much joshing as they can out of the inevitable typing errors which always seem to occur in the performing script. Such lines as "What is that in the road ahead?" are much savoured when they may be presented as "What is that in the road, a head?"

In spite of such good-natured tomfoolery, the experienced actor is able to measure the part which he has to project, and is able to understand the now more real characters with whom he must relate his performance. If the producer is fortunate to have selected a truly professional and experienced cast, his direction will only consist of minor character and speech presentation. All the rest of his expertise will be applied to creating convincing distances, acoustics, pace and general mental imagery for the benefit of the radio audience.

On completion of the initial read-through, the producer will send off the cast and the crew for a canteen break. He, his secretary and the author will then put their heads together for ten minutes or so to discuss any cuts which may be needed to bring the estimated running time down more clearly to that which is required. If the author has done his job well, he will already have considered this to some degree and indicated in his initial script, with squared brackets, where any necessary cuts could be made. With these preliminary changes agreed, the three of you will probably then join the others for some refreshment and a quick chat. And then back to the studio for the hard work.

Each producer has his own particular way of working. One may prefer to rehearse each scene to perfection, then record it and move on to the next scene. Another producer's way might be to rehearse the whole play until he is satisfied, and then record it all in one go. It is merely a matter of personal preference. The writer can recall one occasion on Christmas Eve when all scenes using the female members of the cast were rehearsed first and recorded so that the ladies could scoot away and carry out their Christmas shopping. All very civilised, until it was discovered that one of the actresses had a few words to say in one of the remaining scenes which had been overlooked. Fortunately, by putting a few heads together, it was found possible to 'lift' a few words which she had previously recorded, cut these in to the performance and slightly alter the script accordingly. And nobody in the audience was any the wiser!

We are assuming that it is the BBC which is producing your play, and therefore the aim will be for a high degree of excellence. It should be pointed out that in some parts of the world, such a standard may not be required or even possible. But, generally speaking, radio producers take their work seriously and try to turn out the very best programme they can within the means at their disposal.

Particularly with the BBC, the actors will *act* and not just speak their words. The effects of movement and physical effort to match the dialogue may seem to be quite superfluous to those who have no appreciation of the techniques of radio. But, these effects, subtle as they are, can lift a mediocre production to a considerable height on that score alone.

An actor once had to play the part of a plumber working beneath a kitchen sink, whilst carrying on a conversation with his young mate in the room nearby. The aim was to get a hard, echoey acoustic effect with the plumber's voice from working in a supposedly confined space. The sound engineer added what is known as 'peak' to the output of the microphone being used. But the result was less than perfect. The actor then tried the scene inside a moveable cupboard. The effect was considerably better, but there was a certain 'flatness' in the performance. The plumber sounded as if he were in *any* confined space, when what was desired was the sound of a plumber crunched up under the sink.

It was the actor himself who came up with the perfect solution.

He placed two straightforward chairs just inside the cupboard and lay across them. He also took several pieces of metal from Spotty and holding them above his chest, clattered them together as if he were actually working on a drain pipe. When one lies flat, the diaphragm takes up a different position and affects the breathing and sound of the voice. It is an effect which is almost impossible to achieve when one is in the upright position.

Also, by being able to regulate the metallic sounds himself, the actor was able to build them around his breathing and his lines in a perfectly normal way – something which Spotty could never have done as well.

From this one example, you should now understand that it is possible to include movement, effort, posture and distance into the writing of your radio play. You are *not* constrained to a few people simply speaking into a microphone. You can build a complete and subtle dimension into your work. You can add *life* to the spoken words.

Write one scene with a couple in bed, with a 'soft' acoustic and a gently ticking clock in the background. Then move on to an open street scene early in the morning. The milkman clatters his bottles, a dog yaps a fair way off, there is light traffic and the postman is delivering the mail. Change to the kitchen with the radio in the background. Water splashes in the sink and the kettle rises to a whistling boil. Then out to the platform of a suburban railway station, with the hubbub of waiting passengers, perhaps a station announcement and the sound of a train pulling into the station. Move on to an inside acoustic of a cafeteria, with subdued chatter in the background – the clatter of crocks and cutlery and a few words from the counter assistant to one of your characters. Ring the changes, but keep them within what is reasonable for telling your story.

Remember that the studio staff have to provide *some* acoustic and effects whatever you write. So, you are causing them no extra work at all if you provide them with something worthwhile to create.

Two points should be raised here which should be of considerable help to you in writing your script. The first is that only the most disinterested of radio producers would permit a scene to be recorded with no acoustic at all. It would sound completely dead. Even a scene played against, say, quiet open moorland in the middle of the night something will have to be added. This is usually 'Victoria Falls' or the sound of cascading water played at an extremely low volume. It adds a subtle ssshhhh which can hardly be heard or appreciated, but oh how dead everything seems when it is taken away.

The second point is that you should make full use of minor characters to flesh out your play and give it more substance. When you constructed it, you bore very much in mind that each actor would have to be paid for, so you kept your cast list to the barest minimum – and that could have been a very significant factor in your play being accepted.

So, you are going to make use of minor characters. Before doing so there are certain ground rules which you will have to observe. Staying with our assumption that your play is being produced by the BBC, we should take a look at their method of operation in the field of radio drama.

The BBC repertory company consists of a changing group of actors and actresses, who often work on three year contracts, at fixed salaries, plus overtime at agreed rates of pay. You could say with some degree of accuracy that they move about from studio to studio taking those parts which are considered to be within their acting range.

When your producer has accepted your play, he then has to produce it within the constraints of an overall budget. It would be quite usual for him to try and bring in one or two lead actors to play the parts of the principal characters. This could account for the major part of his expenditure. He would then 'order' the rest of the cast from the repertory company office and be billed for their services in due course on an internal invoice.

What you have to remember is, that you should not plan to use the lead actors for any 'bit' parts. In the first place, it is not considered to be 'good form'. Secondly, it would be nothing short of disaster and result in a complete collapse of the illusion if the radio listener should be able to identify the voice of Lord Nonsuch as also speaking the part of the second footman.

Let your minor characters be played by the actors playing the lesser characters of your play. Also, remember that the actor's union *Equity* would not be at all happy if the BBC were guilty of trying to get too much for nothing. Let your 'bit' characters say only a word or two to indicate their presence, and be of unnamed individuals – telephonists, taxi-drivers, waiters etc.

The producer will most probably have a budget amount to spend over a given number of productions. If he aims to turn out a 'block-buster' or large-cast play from time to time, then he must obviously make some economies over the remainder. And this is a factor which you can use to good advantage as a new scriptwriter. Let your piece be economical in the number of cast. Perhaps you could keep it down to at least four or five members. Then, depending on the nature of your story, fill it out with interesting and varied scenes. Make it 'feel' big by using to the full what you now know about the studio technology. Contrive to have your actors using effort and movement – take them for a walk in the park instead of sitting in a drawing room. Have them at various distances from each other so that they have to call to each other – 'pitch' as it is known in the profession.

Another trick is to use characters whom we never hear. Done with care and imagination, this can be very effective. Such as:

*(INSIDE ACC OF KITCHEN. WASHING-UP ETC)*

MARY: Did you thank Mr. Brown for getting Tibbles out of the tree?

BILL: I ... er ... I forgot.

MARY: Forgot! I ask you! Look, he's out in his garden now.

BILL: *(moving)* Oh, yes.

MARY: Well? Go on – thank him

BILL: Later ... I'll have a word with him later.

MARY: Oh, you! Later, later, later – that's all I ever hear. It's always me that has to do everything, isn't it

*F/X: (OPEN BACK DOOR. SOUND OF LAWN MOWER IN DISTANCE)*

(*pitching*) Mr. Brown! Yoo-hoo! Mr. Brown! Thank you for getting Tibbles down. (*pause*) Yes, he's fine. Thank you again.

*F/X: (CLOSE DOOR AND CUT OUTSIDE B'GROUND)*

MARY: (*normal*) See? It's as easy as that. Why couldn't you do it?

BILL: 'Cos I'm eating my dinner and you told me not to let it get cold.

Do you get the idea? Pure deception!

Crowd scenes can very easily be tailor-made to suit your special requirement. The record library will hold many and various types of group background. They will have these in many languages and of large and small composition. You may have a scene in a Paris café with a light chatter in French and the occasional laugh – or most languages – with music, if you wish to add to it another recording – 'mixed', as it is called. You could have a much larger crowd just as readily. And these backgrounds are simplicity itself to 'doctor'.

Let us suppose, that your play takes place at the time of the French Revolution. There will be no one special effect recording which can give you what you want – and that is a roaring crowd from which can be heard shouts of protest to make your particular point. What would probably happen (if you only knew that you could ask for it) is that the producer would assemble the whole cast and any spare bodies standing around, including you, in front of a microphone and ask you to ad-lib for a few minutes. A recording would be made of you all muttering and mumbling and shouting out the occasional – "Death to the Aristocrats!" – "Off with their heads!" – "Down with the King!" Quite possibly you would do this a few times. Then, the sound engineer would mix these onto another recording tape, and perhaps add another track from the library of a large football crowd.

This may sound very complex, but an experienced sound engineer can work his magic in ten or twenty minutes and give you the most impressive sounds of a stampeding mob and breaking glass and timber (from other recordings). Not only this, but one can distinctly hear what all the protesting is about. This can all be underlying the dialogue of your characters who are perhaps being carried along unwillingly (effort and pitching).

Your overall cast for the play may only be five or six actors, yet you will have achieved in one part and in radio terms, an effect equal to that of a feature film with a cast of thousands.

As you listen to the cast rehearsing and recording, you may find that they will occasionally stumble with your dialogue. You should make particular note of any of these lines and ask yourself if it was in anyway the fault of your script. We writers are all liable to be tempted to aim too high with our dialogue at times. But what we have to remember with radio is that we are closer to film and television than we are to the stage performance. With any of the audio-visual media, our eyes and ears work together and we can take in all combinations of movement and pace in sight and sound. With radio, our ears do all of the work. A skilled radio writer will understand that he must not permit the ear of the listener to become dulled with a sameness of acoustics, special effects, spoken words and, most of all – pace. The pace of the action will quicken when emotions are flaring, and when the author wishes to convince the listener that there is considerable effort and movement.

You will find that you can read aloud any fine piece of classic literature – *if you do so at your own speed.* Try this at two or three times that speed and you will possibly find that these fine words sound as though they are coming from the mouth of a person of moronic tendency, suffering from lockjaw – and eating peanuts and chewing gum at the same time. *When words must be spoken quickly or are supported by effort and movement, those words must be simple, short and far removed from the tongue-twisting kind.*

When a character is supposed to be suffering from physical or mental anguish then his dialogue will tend to be disjointed – incomplete, confused. When you have the opportunity to write this kind of material, then you should do so with gusto and abundance. If you should have overwritten to any great degree, this will be spotted during the rehearsal and trimmed accordingly. In fact, if you are going to make any mistake at all, it will probably be the result of shyness and end in underwriting. Take care to avoid it. Actors love these pieces and will usually throw themselves into the performance as if their life depended on it. But it can look quite strange when written down.

The following piece was spoken by Samuels, a Jewish pawnbroker in RATCLIFFE HIGHWAY – a blood-and-thunder thriller set in the 1800's.

*F/X: (OUTSIDE ACC. NIGHT WITH OCCASIONAL DISTANT CAT. F'STEPS MOVING IN ON COBBLES)*

WATCHMAN: (*moving in – pitching*) Twelve o'clock on a fine cold night. And ... all's ... well! (*coughs and spits*) (*under*) aye! And cold it is!

*F/X (OFF – DOOR THROWN OPEN – BOXES OR CASES FALLING)*

SAMUELS: (*off – sobbing*)

WATCHMAN: (*pitching*) Who be that? Who be ... ?

SAMUELS: (*moving in – hysterical sobs*)

WATCHMAN: (*pitching down*) Who be ... ? Be that you Mr. Samuels?

SAMUELS: (*nearly in*) (*shrieking*) No! No! No!

WATCHMAN: (*down*) Well! Gawd's truth! Here, now – Mr. Samuels!

SAMUELS: (*screams*) Let me go! Let me go!

WATCHMAN: (*sternly*) Mr. Samuels! Sir!!

SAMUELS: (*terrified*) No, don't let me go! Hold me – hold me!

WATCHMAN: What the bloody ... ?

SAMUELS: Take it away! No! Don't let me look! Oh, mother – mother! Oh, my life – the blood – the blood!

WATCHMAN: Blood, you say?

SAMUELS: (*screams*) Don't let me look! Take it away! Take it away! Blood, blood! Their heads – all of them – blood! Go away! Oh, God! God, God, God! Oh, help me someone!

WATCHMAN: Now then!
SAMUELS: (*sobbing*) Their heads! Their throats! Cruel, cruel blood! (*whimpers*) And the baby! Their darling angel baby! I can't ...! I can't ... Oh, God – why? Why? (*sobs*) Baby, baby, baby – darling angel baby. Ohhhh!

On first examination, this piece of script may seem to be terribly overwritten and almost meaningless. But Samuels has, in fact, indicated most strongly what he has just seen without exactly saying so. He is a confused and frightened man at the moment, and his speech is erratic and uses only the most simple of words.

The actor who performed this part was John Gabriel, and when he first acted it into the microphone, he did so with full force and emotion. He also developed the screams, shrieks and whimpers to such a degree that there was hardly one dry hand in the studio. Even the actress eating a cheese roll put down her magazine and took notice!

It is professional pride that makes the actor or actress want to give the best possible interpretation to your characters. You, the writer, owe it to each of them to provide a character with which they can use their skill and artistry. You should ensure that even a small part is a part that is worth playing – and never a matter of being just a piece of convenient furniture. And, don't forget, when you do this you also add to the overall perfection of your piece.

Your play is now all recorded on tape. Its actual playing time should be within a minute or so of the finally required length. Between now and the day of the broadcast, the director and the sound engineer or editor will play it through and trim it down to within a second or two of its required length. This is a subject which could be covered in a book of its own. For the moment, it is sufficient to say that expert editing can achieve considerable economies of length without removing one single word of the final recording. The silences between sentences and even between words can be deftly cut and reduced to give the desired result.

You have seen your first radio play produced and you should now put this experience to good use. Mastery of the skills you have seen demonstrated will not only enable you to write superior material for radio, but to write any material which can be performed by actors. You will be well on your way to being a jack of all trades and the master of them all.

# *Chapter Two*

## THE RADIO SHORT STORY

The radio short story is a short story which is specially written for the spoken voice, and is not just a short story which happens to be read on radio. A failure to understand the essential importance of this fact is probably the principal reason why some very capable writers never hear their stories broadcast over the air.

The only other error that many, many writers commonly make is to submit the wrong *type* of story. Writing for the spoken voice is quite an easy technique to learn. It truly is as simple as falling off a log. When it comes to writing up a suitable *type* of story, some writers can show a measure of obstinacy which can be described as being unbelievably stupid.

You should know, for instance that stories dealing with animals are not at all in demand for adult listening. For children's programmes yes indeed, but not for adults. A typical example of senseless obduracy was the lady who only wanted to write stories about animals and pets. The producer to whom she sent these scripts went to the trouble of telling her several times that he was not in the market for this kind of material. But she decided to contest his advice. She 'couldn't see why' there should be this policy – she claimed that her stories were 'excellent' – and so they were. And she was going to 'make' him accept her work.

Since she lived at some distance from the poor man's office – and since she could hardly put her knee in his chest and crush him into submission – she did the next best thing. She posted to him two stories a month for a number of years. Stories concerning cats, dogs, budgerigars, lambs, horses – the nightmare seemed to go on forever! It sounds incredible that an apparently educated, mature and intelligent woman should devote herself to such a waste of her own time and that of other people in an attempt to 'beat the establishment'.

In passing, it is worth mentioning that not only radio suffers from this kind of writer. Book publishers, stage producers and TV companies are constantly sent material which is quite unsuitable for them – or sometimes for anyone else! After a long time spent getting nowhere, some of these writers begin to see the light of day. Others never do. They just fade away, shouting their protests to the last. It is sad to see such a person being their own worst enemy – when all they needed to do was write a different kind of material.

Anyway, back to our discussion of the radio short story.

You have no doubt read elsewhere that we writers have our roots in the early story-teller. It is easy to conjure up a picture of an elderly bearded man sitting at the camp fire with a ring of faces looking expectantly at him and hanging on to his every word. That is no bad way for you to see yourself as you sit down to write your story. You know that your listener could be in any sort of busy situation when your story is broadcast, but you hope that you can engage his or her attention and hold it to the end.

But, there is no camp fire and we live in a far more sophisticated age. You must have all the magic of basic story-telling, plus the technique of radio presentation. We have already said that many 'ordinary' short stories are not suitable for radio. What we can also say is, that when you have written a story specially for radio – you will also have written a story that will be much better in print than the 'ordinary' one. There is no point in going into this any further. It is a fact that you will discover for yourself.

If you wish to master this particular technique, then you will also find that the discipline of working to a deliberate plan will develop your creative muscles and strengthen your writing abilities for any other area which you wish to try.

Either completely or partially, you have your story in mind. You first have to determine its length. For a fifteen-minute programme, an ideal length would be 2,150 words. Bearing in mind that we said about cutting and trimming of the radio play, you would be well advised to make it about 75 or 100 words longer. And, before you submit it, find some words or paragraphs which you can mark with square brackets as *your* choice of proposed trims.

Your story will be read by a professional actor or actress. Before you start writing, you must decide which of these it is to be, because that will determine how the story must be told. Should it be a young reader – or of more advanced years? Well-spoken, or closer to Mother Earth? Then the nationality or dialect have to be fixed on. All important factors to be decided before you can really put a word to paper – because you are going to build another dimension into your work – your story is going to be *acted.* And that is what you are going to write – a part for an actor which is also a short story.

As a professional, your reader will relish the opportunity to have one or two 'parts' to play within your story. This is character acting within the overall acted piece. This may seem somewhat complicated in description, but you will soon understand what is meant.

Let us suppose that you write your story to be told be a middle-aged middle-class lady, and she is telling us about a 'war' which takes place in her house between her elderly mother and the District Nurse. For the main narrative, the actress will be just what you want her to be – a middle-age middle-class lady. When she speaks as Grannie, her voice will perhaps drop and become a little gravelly – she may possibly be a trifle waspish.

In a *written* story you could say: "Where have you been? I've been on my own for hours!" Grannie said waspishly. For a written story, that would be just fine. But, your actress will *say* this piece of dialogue waspishly, so you do not need to write waspishly. You only write down – she said. It is worth spending a moment or two to get that clearly understood before moving on.

Now, for the District Nurse. You would want her to be as different as possible to the middle-aged lady and her mother – but within the range of the reader's capabilities. You could decide to make her in her early thirties and Irish born. You would not put these facts in your manuscript as stage directions, but the same as you would in any short story. Your middle-aged lady could say: Within the next few minutes, Nurse Rooney would arrive, bringing with her Grannie's medicine, her young enthusiasm and more than a touch of Irish Blarney. Any one of which were guaranteed to bring Grannie's guns up to the firing position.

So, your short story has, in fact, now become something of a playlet – with three spoken voices.

But what if your story does not have a District Nurse? Your third character is Grandad. How can your reader speak with her own voice, Grannie's voice, and the male voice of an elderly man? Well, she doesn't need to – because you paraphrase what Grandad says so that we don't actually hear him.

Something like this:

Grannie stared at me closely as I forced down the second piece of fruit cake. "You're too thin, girl," she said. "If you don't put on some more weight, you'll sicken for something!" She turned sharply towards Grandad and, almost as a challenge, said – "She'll sicken for something, won't she?"

Grandad rattled his newspaper and buried his head deeper with a mumbled word. He agreed with her up to a point, but this was no battle that he was going to volunteer into.

We have all that we need of Grandad's response, but the actress did not need to play his part.

So you see how important it is to fit your story to the reader and the reader to the story at the same time when writing for radio.

We now come to the question of what is a suitable kind of story for radio, and to find the answer we have to consider some more background. Who is likely to listen to this story?

The answer is, almost anyone. A mechanic working under a car could have his transistor radio on. A hospital patient recovering from major surgery could be wearing earphones. Service-men and mariners on the high seas often listen to radio. And then there are all the other listeners in millions of situations involved in thousands of different activities. This is the potential audience of the radio short story producer who has the almost impossible task of finding something which appeals to everyone.

That may seem to be an impossibility of the highest order, but it can be done to a very considerable extent by eliminating the main *categories* of fiction. Take crime stories, for example. You may feel that by not broadcasting crime stories, the producer has not satisfied those listeners who prefer crime stories. That may be perfectly true but, at the same time, he has not caused those listeners who can not bear crime stories at any price to switch off.

It stands to reason that if he does not use anything which would automatically cause people to switch off, then he has kept them listening in. And that is the whole reasoning behind the selection of stories.

It is no to crime, detection, pure romance, ghost stories, fantasy and horror. It is no to pet and animal stories which would set on edge the teeth of hairy-armed sailors and with-it teenagers. It is no-no to anything crude, scarey or naughty.

Here we must mention again the lady who wanted to solve the world's problems by writing animal stories. She wanted to break down what she considered to be an unreasonable resistance to accepting them. She was absolutely convinced that there were many listeners who would be interested in her stories. She just could not accept the fact her personally-motivated arguments were as nothing compared to the reasoning and decision bearing on the main issue – which was the use of material which would appeal to most listeners.

We have indicated what type of story is *not* suitable, and that is any story which fits into a definite and specialised category. This means that suitable short stories for radio are, by the process of elimination, those which are of a general character. And, if you listen to those which are regularly broadcast, this will prove to be the case.

You will find that these stories also take the middle ground between high comedy and heavy drama. By that we do not mean that they are of a neutral character, but contain both the elements of humour and drama to a lighter degree. If you like – the unvarnished truth about people, told with a smile.

The novice writer could feel that he now has no area in which to find an idea for a story, but he would be quite wrong. Suitable story ideas are far easier to think up than he would first believe. It just takes a little knack. And, as with all knacks, it is just a matter of applying one's powers of thought to it when, suddenly, everything drops into place.

It is now time to put all these points concerning the short story together and check if they do, in fact, work.

Read the following radio short story first. Then go through it again slowly and see if you can pick out where the author has used radio technique to achieve the desired effect.

## THE MAGIC TOUCH

*Reader's Note:* Carlos speaks with marked Italian accent.

Carlos Vella's podgy little fingers ran across the trays of pizza pies, weaving patterns of anchovy with the certainty of fifty years experience. Then followed the shining black olives, each one appearing out his age-spotted fist with a faint 'plop' and leaping into the waiting bed of grated cheese.

Behind him the restaurant door swung open under the manicured hand of his son, Angelo. Impatient noises came from Angelo's throat and his immaculate moustache twitched with annoyance. "How much longer will you be, Father?" he asked. "We've been waiting for you for nearly an hour."

Carlos took a long and appreciative sniff at the yeasty-smelling pizza. "Soon, Angelo. Soon I come in. Unless – you and your brothers, and your wives, they all like to come and talk in the kitchen, Eh? What you say?"

Angelo flicked an offending speck of flour from his tailor-made sleeve. "Thank you, Father, no. The kitchen is not the place for important business ... important *family* business", [he added with emphasis]

Carlos smiled broadly and threw up his hands in mock horror to the tiled walls, even to the burnished copper soup kettles.

"Oho! This no place for the business, you say? Where else the food business if not in the kitchen? Back forty years I bring your Mamma to England. Thirty years she help me here. This where I start the business. What you mean, this no place for the business?"

"Let's not go into that again," Angelo said, "you know what I mean."

And only too well *did* Carlos know. None of them were at ease in the warm womb of the kitchen; they felt at a disadvantage.

Not that Carlos ever wanted it that way. Far, far from it. But the plain fact was, that neither Angelo, nor his middle-aged brothers, nor any of their wives wanted anything to do with Italian cooking. From top to toe, inside out, they were all thoroughly, positively British.

An ordinary Italian chef might have died from shame. But not Carlos Vella. He happened to be more than an ordinary Italian chef; he was the acknowledged expert, a master, and not far short of a magician with your taste buds. He wasn't shamed. They were his family. And he was tolerant. And he had enough skill for all of them.

Wiping the olive brine from his hands, he reached to his full height of five-foot-three, and swam his hand around in a cupboard for a jar of sweet-smelling marjoram.

The fingers knew what they touched as surely as if they could see. This the bay leaves – that the mint – rosemary – tarragon – and, over here, the allspice – to the right, the paprika – the nutmeg. And, suddenly, this! What was this? The fingers, now confused, clutched at a strange shape and drew it to within a few inches from his nose.

It was a pack of playing cards, linen finish, all splashed with bright red and gold. Ah! What luck he should find them again today! Tonight, the customers will see them. And how they will see them! He will borrow a handkerchief and produce the cards magically from it. Fanned out wide, they will be a sight to be remembered. Then, they must disappear up his sleeve, one at a time. And then ... The evening-to-be was shattered by the voice of Angelo.

"Will you please hurry up! Some of us have important engagements. We can't wait about all day."

Carlos held up the cards. "You see, Angelo? Your Nicky, he give me these for Christmas."

Angelo's nose pinched as if to a bad smell. "For the last time, will you please come into the restaurant!" He turned and left the kitchen without even looking at the cards.

Sadly, Carlos wagged his head. Angelo was a big boy now. Forty-three? Or was it forty-five years old? Which ever it was, he was old enough to be more patient. All this hurrying – got to do it now – quick, quick – the meetings – the important engagements. If he had to do so many things, better he got up earlier in the morning and not rush himself into a bad temper. But, they *had* all come to see him. That was nice. So, we say hello and let them get to their important engagements.

He found the marjoram and measured a bare spoonful into a cup. He added the same amounts of basil and thyme and a pinch, the barest pinch, of the tangy cardamom. Clapping his hand over the cup, he shook the herbs and spice until they burst out, a pungent-sweet cloud, over the pies. He was finished; the yeast would carry on the work while he sat with his family.

He went to the sink. Through the window he could see the backyard. When Mamma was alive she grew his herbs out there. And always, in the summer, when the last customer had finished lunch and the dishes were washed, she sat there knitting jumpers for the boys. But not now. No mint grew in the corner. No chives pushed their green needles through the layer of cinders that the boys had ordered. Now it was for the cars. 'For the use of the proprietors only' their notice said. It *still* didn't sound very nice English to Carlos, but Angelo insisted that was what you had to say – and, with the cost of the school he went to, he should know.

Four cars waited there now, all black and shiney, with important-looking buttons and knobs that convinced Carlos, with his little education, that he would never have the wits to learn how to drive. It would be good if the little red car was there now; the one he had bought for his grandson Nicky. Nicky, the giver of those beautiful red and gold cards at Christmas. Nicky, son of Angelo – the oh, so impatient Angelo.

Alright, so Nicky hadn't come today. He would come again soon. He always did.

Carlos swished his hands under the tap, then waddled off to the restaurant.

His four sons and their wives sat stiffly at the linen-covered tables, their stern eyes guiding him to the straight-backed chair they had placed under the brightest light in the place.

Carlos settled his ample little body onto the chair, removed his chef's hat, folded his hands across his middle, and smiled at them all. The barest suggestion of a smile came back to him.

As gracefully as a cat, Angelo moved a chair forward and sat facing his father. Just a little closer to him than the others, but not close enough to suggest that he was leaving his own team. As usual, he would be spokesman.

He leaned forward and drew together his eyebrows in the way that never failed to give Carlos a thrill of fatherly pride. From an expensive briefcase he took a sheet of ledger paper covered with precise columns of figures.

"Father," he said, "the business is going down hill. And we have all come here today because something must be done about it."

Carlos picked up a menu and ran his eyes down the right-hand side. Three times this year they had increased the charges. He sucked in his cheeks. Three times is a lot of times. When he first came to London he gave a whole five-course meal for the price of today's minnestroni. The food here was the best, of course. But a meal is only a meal. Because you have that extra touch doesn't mean you should be a robber. Knowing *when* to use caramel, knowing *how much* garlic was enough, knowing *what* pepper to put into *which* soup – these things didn't give a man the right to pluck his regular customers clean.

But, down hill Angelo said, and something must be done.

He rehearsed the words before he spoke them. Angelo would be pleased that he, too, could speak this business business. "O.K. We print the new menu. Everything goes up the ten percent."

Angelo's face remained unmoved.

Carlos added quickly, "And we make the two-and-a-half percent for the service cover."

Angelo tapped the paper with his gold fountain pen. "Until three years ago, Father, this business was a gold mine. Now it's not. There used to be a good living for all of us. Now . . .!" and he pointed the accusing pen at Carlos. "What happened three years ago?"

Carlos searched through the cluttered attic of his memory. Did they buy the new restaurant carpet then? No, that was before – Mamma chose that. Guaranteed ten years wear, she said. More like twenty it would be. She was always careful to get value. Was it the cinders in the car park? No, they came out of the money he decided not to waste on a holiday without Mamma. Three years ago! Ah, now he remembered! "Three years ago," he told Angelo, "three years ago we had the new government. Every time we have the new government – we don't make the money."

Angelo shook his head. "Three years ago, Father, you started doing card tricks." He paused while the rest of the family nodded solemnly.

Carlos considered for a moment. Had he been wasting money? He didn't think so. There was the book, of course – Card Magic For Beginners. That cost a lot. He paid over a pound for that. But it came out of his own post office book. And three packs of cards. No, two packs – the red and gold ones came free – from young Nicky – for Christmas.

"All I spend on the magic is under the two pounds," he explained.

"It's not how much you spend that we mind," Angelo said, "you are perfectly entitled to spend all of your money as you please. What we are saying is that the takings are down by thirty percent. And we think we know why."

Once again the accusing pen pointed at Carlos. "The takings are down, Father, because you spend more time on your card tricks than you do preparing food. The customers are being driven away by the slow service."

Angelo moved his chair back slightly to make a common front with the others. "We have all decided," he said, "that you can not both cook and conjure. The two things don't mix. And we are worried – very worried."

Carlos smiled happily. At least, they were worried for him. They were actually worried for him!

"That's right," he said, "nobody can do the two things at the same time. Sometimes the man's got to choose what's the more important. When he gets to be the old man, lik'a me, he's not got the time to waste. You're right, Angelo. I finish with the restaurant business. I close it down – sell out."

One, two, three, four – eight jaws dropped in shocked surprise.

Angelo moved nearer to his father. He put away the gold pen and forced a smile. "We can't force you to work, Father," he said, "but the restaurant has been your whole life. There's no sense in throwing it away. It's become an institution. Customers come for miles. You can't let them down, can you? It wouldn't be fair. Not to anyone, would it? Your own recipes, your special touch, they mustn't be lost. No, you must find another chef and train him."

Carlos reached out and patted Angelo's hand. "These things you can't teach to strangers," he said, "they grow. From the father to the son. In the blood. Working together. And if the sons are too busy to do the work, how they going to learn? A long, long time back I ask you boys to come in the kitchen. Now it's too late. The card tricks you can learn any old time. Cooking, cooking my way, you got to start when you're young."

The silence that followed was broken by a tapping at the street door. Carlos opened it. Nicky stood outside. He wanted to know if Grandad needed any help.

Carlos squeezed Nickey's arm and returned to the high-backed chair under the brightest light in the place. He perched his chef's hat on his pink, bald head.

"You tell me, Nicky," he said, "how you like your old Grandad tell you all his secrets? Give you the magic touch. Make you the expert in the family. How you like the idea?"

Nicky liked the idea very much.

Carlos turned to his sons and their wives. "All my life I look after the family. Another two years, maybe three, I give Nicky the business. Then I don't get the money to look after the family no more. Maybe Nicky, he's got his own family by then. He look after them. He look after me."

Carlos took his grandson into the kitchen and sat him at the table. "One more hour we got before we open for the lunch," he said, "so now I give you the first lesson. Get you set up for the good life."

He reached into the spice cupboard and brought out a packet which he emptied onto the table. The red and gold backs of the cards were like a blazing fire.

"You listen good, Nicky," Carlos said. "Lesson number one – how to make the cards vanish up the sleeve."

*Reprinted by permission of FACT & FICTION AGENCY LTD*

This story was broadcast three times by the BBC, and has been sold many times around the world. It has also been included in one book, and has been used as the basis for a full-length radio play.

It is a simple story, simply told. True, it has a twist in the tail – and this could be part of its success, but if you will study it closely, you will find that it is constructed solidly on the radio techniques which are described earlier in this chapter.

The BBC chose that fine actor, Robert Rietty to give it its first performance. For the narrative, he used his own well-modulated voice. For Angelo, he was crisp, nasal and very, very British. As Carlos, he was so Italian that you could almost smell'a da spaghetti!

# Chapter Three

## THE RADIO PLAY

If there were only one piece of advice that could be given to the aspiring radio playwright, then that advice should be – *For God's sake write a play that goes somewhere!*

The only place that most radio plays which are submitted to go – is straight back to the author.

Just occasionally, you will hear a radio play whose obvious intent is to inform or to provoke the listener to thought. You will also find that these pieces are written with considerable artistry and will be considered to be entertaining *for those people who enjoy that sort of thing*. It is only right and proper that radio should make air-space available for these kinds of plays, and our work-aday world would be the poorer without them.

Nevertheless – as we wish to be as honest as possible – there are many, many listeners who do not wish to be involved in making any other contribution to that play other than just being near to the radio. There will be occasions when you will be of the same mind yourself. *You just want to be entertained.*

So, these think-piece plays as we may call them, do tend to be in the minority. We can also shovel in with them that inevitable kind of strange play which, by its power of words and the artistry of the actors, holds you spellbound as if you were about to have revealed to you the basic secret of existence – and you find that at the end of the play you have a handful of nothing. It can leave you with a strange feeling – almost as if you had been mocked and cheated. Plays without ends come under this heading, too.

If any play of this nature should happen to be broadcast, believe me it will be the exception and not the rule.

Your best chance of having a play accepted is to write a story that goes somewhere. Someone or something has changed during the telling of this tale. And you are courageous enough to spell it out in no uncertain terms. The only imagination you require from the listener is to provide the pictures in his mind from the sounds which you provide. There really is no mystique to all this. If you want to break into radio drama, then just don your long whiskers and become a good old storyteller. Leave the think-pieces and the tub-thumping until you are well established.

All right, you have an idea for a play which is going to have popular appeal and will go somewhere. On hearing it, your listener will be left with the feeling that he has been well repaid for giving you his time. He may even write in to the company and tell them so.

You are going to submit a manuscript which is so professionally put together that it just begs to be accepted.

The first decision you have to make is to settle on its approximate length. There will occasionally be a slot for fifteen-minute plays, but these do not constitute the main stream of drama productions. The thirty-minute play is often to be heard, but you should not assume that the short play is best for the beginner.

It is so easy to say to oneself: – "Ah, I will start with a thirty-minute play. Then, as I become more experienced, I will move up to the sixty-minuter. And when I have won my crown, I shall write ninety-minute plays." It is not as easy as that. Very often, the thirty-minute play can be the most difficult of all. You have very little elbow-room in which to create three-dimensional characters for example.

You should make a point of listening to a thirty-minute radio programme – *any* programme – music, comedy, current affairs – anything will serve. As it ends, just cast your mind back to the beginning, and you will appreciate how short that thirty minutes has been.

A certain amount of time will be taken up by the lead-in announcement, and by the trail out and credits. There will be brief pauses in the dialogue and between scenes. A little time will also be given to special effects, we may suppose. You now have less than that thirty minutes for your characters to speak. Let us say twenty-six minutes.

If you used four characters with which to tell your story – then each of them will have, on average, six-and-a-half minutes each in which to project themselves.

Now, moving away from radio writing for the moment – let us assume that you are at home, and there is a knock at your door.

You open it to discover there a man who wants to sell you double-glazing. Naturally, your first reaction is to tell him no thank you. He then offers to leave a leaflet with you; explains that everyone except you in your street has been bright enough to take advantage of his service, and then permits you to close your door. You go back to your comfortable armchair or ironing board and discover that six-and-a-half minutes of your time have passed. Just how much information did you get from that man? And how well did you get to know him as a person? Not very much, that is for sure. And you even had the advantage of seeing him in the flesh, and watching his physical mannerisms.

There is a very old truism in this writing game of ours. It is that, as a high ideal, every word that you write should serve one of four purposes. And they are:

TO MOVE THE STORY FORWARD
TO REVEAL CHARACTER
TO CREATE ATMOSPHERE
TO CAUSE A LAUGH

With radio and TV writing, this becomes more than an ideal – it is an essential requirement – and particularly when you are dealing with the shorter length.

As a rule of thumb, we can say that when we write a half-hour radio play we must choose which of the above-mentioned factors will get the lion's share of the words. Which means that you will concentrate on the STORY or CHARACTER or ATMOSPHERE or LAUGHS. Therefore, the ideal material for the half-hour length will be that which has a strong story which can be quickly told, or a story whose strength is in characterization.

There will sometimes be a spot for the 45-minute drama play but, once again, this is not the most popular length.

To some degree, we have to consider the work of the programme planners, whose function it is to arrange the day's broadcasting programme. This is done by the clock. Presumably, they find it convenient to have programmes which are in multiples of a quarter of an hour.

At any rate, the one-hour radio play is the one which is mostly used, and that is the one on which we should set our sights. It gives us the best opportunity of acceptance, being of a length which enables us to tell a satisfying story, with enough time in which to create a convincing atmosphere peopled by three-dimensional characters that will really come to life for the listener.

A further advantage of the one-hour play is that it will often get a mid-week repeat on the network and be of interest to broadcasting companies in other countries – if you have chosen your subject well.

The longest time for a radio play would probably be ninety minutes, and these can often be heard. But this length requires almost as much *story* as two one-hour plays, and many writers would, in fact, prefer to write two one-hour plays than one of ninety minutes. It is a convenient length when you have something of an epic or historical subject, and many classical stage plays find their way into this spot.

So, you have your subject and your probable length – which we will assume to be of sixty minutes. And you are ready to start your journey into the unknown.

You would certainly feel more secure and confident if you were provided with a map of where you are going, and providing this map should be your first activity.

Your play will consist of separate scenes, which you will vary in pace, content and atmosphere, as we have already discussed, in order to hold the interest of the listener. An ideal length of scene is three minutes. This gives you enough time to develop some piece of action or show some character in action – but it is not really long enough to become boring.

You therefore have the loose intention of mapping out your story into twenty scenes of three minutes each. We say the loose intention, because this is no holy law, but a point from which you can start to plan. You may end up with twelve scenes, or thirty. Some scenes may be only thirty seconds long, or ten minutes. It doesn't really matter, just as long as you have an idea from where you start.

Sometimes the map that you need will fall into place in no time at all, particularly if you have been continually turning it over in your mind. Or it could take a considerable amount of stretching, bending and changing in order to get a well-formed framework on which you can now hang your words and characters. But do remember, even once you are well into the writing of the play, that your map is only a guide. Often far better ideas come up in the writing, and you would be foolish to ignore them.

Armed with your map, you now commence to write your play. You will be pleased to know that the first few words that you write have already been decided for you. Well, to be more precise – the *words* have not been decided – but what those first few words must achieve is quite obligatory.

In as short a possible time – certainly within a minute or so – you must indicate who, where and when.

In the early days of radio drama, it was quite usual for the announcer to 'set-up' the situation for the benefit of the listener. Something like this: –

"Our play this evening begins with Colonel Bogey of the Royal Standback Fusiliers taking breakfast with his wife on the verandah of their villa at the Indian town of Poona during the early part of the year eighteen, ninety-two."

You can't do that these days. Every piece of information has to come out of the words of the characters. And what is more, it must not appear to do so. You cannot, for example, have an actor begin the play by saying: –

"Tell me, my darling wife Mildred – is it still the sixteenth of May, nineteen seventy-six? And is your mother who lives in Bradford coming down here to Devon to stay with us for two weeks?"

No, you can't do that, either. You have to achieve the same result by far more subtle means, also indicating character and other significances at the same time. You would have to write something like this:

F/X: *(INSIDE KITCHEN ACC. RADIO PROG OFF COOKING UTENSILS)*
MILDRED: (*pitching – off*) Gerald!
GERALD: (*pitching – off*) Hello?
MILDRED: Breakfast – on the table.
GERALD: Coming. *(pause)* I was looking for my cheque book.
MILDRED: You left it on the ...
GERALD: Yes, I found it, thanks. Must get to the bank. Should have paid this bill by the sixteenth of May.
MILDRED: That's only today.
GERALD: Yes, but ...
MILDRED: Now, stop worrying. And you've got plenty of time to go to the bank. Mother isn't leaving Bradford until nine o'clock this morning.
GERALD: If she catches the express ...
MILDRED: She still won't be here 'til tea-time.
GERALD: And I still haven't found that monkey-puzzle plant she wanted.
MILDRED: Oh, for goodness sake! She's staying for two weeks, remember. There must be a hundred nurseries in Devon. She'll probably welcome the chance to go looking for herself.
GERALD: I don't know if I can spare the time.

MILDRED: Then let her take the car, and leave her to it.
GERALD: Oh, my God!
MILDRED: What now?
GERALD: I've just remembered ... I didn't get the wing-mirror fixed. And I have to go to the bank. And ...
MILDRED: Gerald! Now stop that! It isn't necessary. She's my mother, and I should know. She's the gentlest, the kindest, dear sweet soul that ever trod the earth. You're not going to say you're afraid of her, are you?
GERALD: No, Mildred. *(under breath)* Afraid of her? My, God – I'm bloody terrified of her.

This short piece of conversation has imparted to the listener all of the information that we previously mentioned, and has done so with subtlety. It also *feels* like normal conversation. We get the impression that Gerald is something of a ditherer and, rightly or wrongly, is not at ease in the company of his mother-in-law. Whilst Mildred is not exactly a dragon, we suppose that she can be firm of purpose and perhaps 'wears the trousers' in this house.

All right, we know that the beginning of your first scene must have a definite purpose – and that is to quickly introduce the characters in a time, in a place and in a situation.

It would be all too easy to suppose that all further scenes in your play should be handled exactly in the same way – but you now have to play the game slightly differently.

Before you write a scene, you should make a brief note of the *purpose* of that scene. If it doesn't have a purpose, then it has no place in your play – it is going to be padding – chewing-gum for the earholes. We come back to what we previously said about words. The purpose of your scene should be to:

MOVE THE STORY FORWARD
REVEAL CHARACTER
CREATE ATMOSPHERE
CAUSE A LAUGH

– or a combination of these factors.

You will have heard that a story should have a beginning, a middle and an end. This rule, of course, applies just as much to your radio play. And we can further use this advice by saying that each of your scenes should have a beginning, a middle and an end. We can bend this rule to a tiny degree, when we 'fade in' to a scene, and the beginning is not so clearly defined. But the middle of your scene must contain real meat. And the end of each of your scenes must complete the purpose that you designed for it.

That does not mean that you should finish each scene at a high dramatic pitch, with the peasants revolting or the husband strangling his wife. But it does mean that the listener must feel that the scene was of great importance to the play and that it ended on a note of definite significance to him.

We now mention a ploy which you will be able to use to very good dramatic purpose, and which is the most important dodge for building tension and maintaining interest that can be used.

We have already said that you should aim to keep your scene to an ideal length of three minutes. What do you do if you have a much longer scene which has a strong end? The answer is – to cut it into two scenes, with an entirely different scene sandwiched in between.

Your first idea was to have your hero confronted by a police officer who, to the surprise of the audience, charges him with some crime and then carries him off to the cop-shop. It looks as though this scene is going to run for five minutes or so.

Instead, you write the first part of this action up to the point where the police officer announces that he is placing the hero under arrest. That leaves your audience with a lovely question mark hanging in the air, doesn't it? And you have abided by the rule of having a purpose for this scene. And the end of the scene certainly has significance and purpose.

With some careful thought on your part, the 'sandwich' scene can serve a multiplicity of purposes, whilst at the same time seeming to be quite innocuous. The hero has been charged with some unstated crime, and we are all wondering what the devil it can be. Your 'sandwich' scene could then be the information that the hero is to be promoted to Area Sales Manager. He does have a driving license, doesn't he? Yes, he does? Oh, gosh – we ask ourselves – will he lose this promotion opportunity because of this police trouble?

The biggest mistake that you could make when you move on to the next scene is to take the threat out of it by saying, for instance, that the offence was only one of parking on a yellow line. The listener does not care for you to build up his interest for a letdown. In writing, you can do a lot of cheating, but this is one area where you must always satisfy the expectations of the listener. There is a little more to this, which we will take up again later in this book.

So, you write your play scene by scene until you reach the end.

Ends can be very bothersome to the new writer, but he can resolve this difficulty to a large degree if he will substitute for the word 'end' the word 'satisfaction'. Instead of saying "This is the end of my story" let him say "This is the satisfaction of my story". Or, using this transposition in a different way, instead of "How do I bring this story to an end" let him try "How do I bring this story to a satisfaction."

It would seem to be a truism that an end cannot be arrived at until the story has been written, but that is not a concrete fact. You will sometimes find that the end of the story is the first 'germ' from which you start, and you go on to create a sequence of events which will satisfactorily bring you to that end.

A little trick of the professional writer is to ask himself if the idea for his ending is, in fact, contained within the beginning of his story. We see this at its most obvious when we have a crime story. A dead body is found, and the question is – who was responsible for that dead body? The end is the answer to that question. Many, many other types of stories can be evolved which work along these same lines – although dead bodies are not involved.

As a development of this principle of finding the end within this beginning, you can write the whole story – find that the end isn't what you want it to be – then change the beginning to give you a satisfactory ending.

Another technique to have up your sleeve, is the possibility of shuffling your scenes around into a different order from that in which you first wrote them. For example:

*Scene 1.* Harry's landlady tells him that he must vacate his room.

*Scene 2.* Harry is looking for another room to rent.

If you transpose these two scenes, then you are into an entirely different area of plot and Harry's reaction to outside influences. Just think it over for a moment, and ask yourself how Harry would feel in the two different circumstances.

We started this chapter by saying that you were going to write a 'map' of where your story was going to take you. If you have taken notice of the tips which have been given to you so far, and if you have written the best that is in you – then you should find that this 'map' is going to be very close to a manuscript which can be submitted for acceptance.

So far, you will probably have been concentrating on the story content, the radio technique, and ways of holding your potential audience interest. And you will probably find that your story characters have developed into very real people in your mind's eye.

If you have any more work to do then it will most likely be in ensuring that your characters are consistent in the opinion of the listener, and in polishing these shadow people into real flesh and blood.

Time spent on making real people out of fictional characters is time well spent, in whatever field you are writing. It can truly be said that characters make your story. If you have read the works of Charles Dickens or Robert Louis Stevenson, you may still have some difficulty in remembering the plot details, or who appeared in which book. But you would have no difficulty in remembering the *characters* of Mr. Micawber – or Long John Silver – or Ben Gunn – or Mr. Bumble. The actual volume of written words involving these four characters would possibly fill no more than forty or fifty pages, yet for many these fictional characters have more solidity and reality than many of the colourless creatures they come into contact with regularly in their daily lives.

It might seem a little frightening that figments of somebody's imagination could be brought out and made to occupy such a significant place in our culture, but it is an inescapable fact. You are not being challenged to create a Mr. Micawber or Oliver Twist for your play, but you are being asked to realise that it is possible to make a fictional character who can be very, very real. It is not all that difficult a task. All that it requires is for you to understand that it is possible, and that you are probably far more capable of pulling it off than you would at first suppose.

You should make a list of your characters in descending order of importance – right down to the last doorman with his "Good morning, madam." Then spend a moment or two considering your main character as a real live person. Ask yourself which actor or actress you would like to hear play this part. This will help you to have a visual picture of the character. Then, go through your play and read every word which is spoken by this character. You will possibly find that some lines now seem to be 'out-of-character'. You may even find that there is a kind of flatness which does not fluctuate according to the emotional ebb and flow of your play. You may find that it is quite the reverse; you have aimed to portray a calm and unruffled individual – yet the lines go up and down the emotional scale like a rubber ball.

Then go through the rest of the characters, one by one, until you have them all nicely compartmented into consistent personalities.

When you have done this, go through the play again slowly, taking particular note of how each of the characters responds to contact with every other character. Here you could find that you may have made the error of letting your people get away with making speeches to one another. What you are looking for is slightly larger than life two-way conversation. We all know that in real life, there is an activity known as 'cocktail conversation' where nobody is even listening to anyone else, yet alone responding in an intelligent way. This has no place in your play, unless you decide that it is essential to have a cocktail party scene, in which you wish to present it for dramatic purpose. If you have no cocktail party, then get away from it completely – because it is the kiss of death.

Conversation between two characters is the easiest dialogue that you will have to write. Conversation between a group of three or more involves the use of your imagination to keep them all 'on-stage' during the scene. Remember that your listeners cannot see the cast which is present as well as you can, therefore you must make it easy for them to know who is present. It is an easy knack to acquire with a little practice – but don't dodge it, because some of the finest radio dialogue you are ever going to write will use three or more characters.

In mathematical terms you can state this as the following number of communications: A-B, A-C, A-BC, BC-A, B-A, B-C, B-AC, AC-B, C-A, C-B, C-AB, AB-C. That makes twelve possibilities of reaction – even if they are all in agreement.

Looked at this way, you will readily appreciate that the three-handed conversation can give you umpteen opportunities in which to portray character and storyline. The main error which you can easily make with the three-hander is to start your scene with two of the characters speaking, and not making the listener aware that a third person is present. Because, when that third person speaks up, it comes as something of a shock.

A normal reaction to hearing this is to say, "Who the devil is that?" Or, "Where did he come from?" To get over this problem, you can start off with two characters together, then have the other one 'move-in' with some kind of natural introduction.

Another point to watch for, is where the third character moves in, says his piece, and has nothing more to say in that scene. What you do here is to let him have his say, then move him out in a convincing way. If you neglect to do this, then you will have given the listener a 'picture' of him standing there like a dummy. Always find means of letting the listener know how many characters are present at one time.

Only have your character hold a telephone conversation if it is absolutely essential. All too often a scriptwriter will use this as an easy way out. A little thought should enable you to find some other way than this. And if you *must* have telephone conversation, then you must be consistent when you use more than one in your play. The firm decision that you have to make is – do we hear the person at the other end of the line? Only you can determine that. We hear the other person (with distorted voice) or we don't. Whichever method you use – you must use for *all* of the telephone calls.

Having only one person on stage can present you with considerable difficulties at times. Let us say right now, that listening in to that person's thoughts, or having him talking to himself can only convincingly be used on rare occasions and only in a few kind of plays. With radio drama, you are trying to build the image of *reality*; real live stuff. And how much mind-reading do you go in for in your life? And if you heard a real person muttering to himself, would you really feel like trusting him with your car or your daughter? This is what can happen. You may be trying to build a sane character that we can relate to. Then you shouldn't take the slightest risk of that character seeming to have a few tiles loose on his roof.

It is also almost impossible to have a single person engaged in some forms of *action* when you are writing for radio. Just how convincingly *can* you portray your character crashing through the woods at midnight, or repairing a timber fence? Not very well, that is for sure. Of course you can use special effects. But special effects are only effective when they are a background to spoken dramatic action. If you had your hero panting and gasping, plus the rustle of leaves and breaking of twigs – then he may just as easily sound as if he were wrapping his Christmas presents whilst suffering from a bad bout of bronchitis. And that is how it could sound over a decent radio set. Heard through a tiny transistor receiver, it could well have the listener believe that he should buy some new batteries.

By now, you should have made up your mind that radio drama really needs to handle two-person situations as the minimum. Do this consistently and you should have no difficulties in achieving the effect of reality.

But what do you do when a character had a lone experience which it is essential to reveal to the listener? The simple answer is that you *tell* it and don't *act* it. In the previous chapter dealing with the radio short story, we paraphrased Grandad's words. We put the information over in a different form. This is what you do with the lone action.

For the purpose of putting across a number of points in this book, we have used as examples stories and actions which are large and bustling. Not all radio drama is of sound and fury. Not all stories deal with sharply defined characters which are completely black or white. Very few of them will use the whole of the record library for special effects. The mainstream of radio plays are played in a much lower key, and most of their charm and appeal comes from a beautiful story concerning people such as ourselves. The 'ordinariness' which is their strong appeal usually runs dangerously close to the line of dullness and mediocrity. It is whether or not a play stays on the right side of this line which determines whether it is bought, or simply returned with thanks. Understanding and using radio technique is what can tip the scales in your favour – every time.

# *Chapter Four*

## THE RADIO SERIAL

Radio serials are very much a law unto themselves, but for our immediate purpose we shall categorise them as short serials and long serials.

The long serial is the one which becomes established almost as a way of life, and causes public outcry if one of the characters should be killed off. Sometimes it may be difficult for us to decide if we should call this drama or fictional documentary, as it tends to move in the same time as ourselves. One of the characters says that "the cows be snowed in" – then we look out of our window and find, sure enough, that we have snow as well. A 'flu epidemic confines us to our bed and, in need of something more exciting than wet paper tissues, we switch on the radio and discover that half the cast is nearer to death than we are ourselves. Their doctor assures them all that they will be on their feet again within three months and we count ourselves lucky that we are made of stronger stuff.

These long serials usually develop from an original short serial, and eventually require a team of scriptwriters to inject new ideas, new enthusiasms and new epidemics into them. Quite often, the original author will carry on by acting as script editor for the programme. A beginner at scriptwriting should not directly aim to become part of such a writing team – although some such talent may be spotted in other scripts which he has submitted, and he could be invited to try his hand at such a programme. Without in any way wishing to underrate the team writers on these shows – it must be said that it is to some extent 'sausage-machine' writing and often not very satisfying to the intensely creative writer with a strong talent and imagination of his own. To be part of such a team would give one quite valuable experience, but there might be a high price to be paid in the form of acquiring a mechanistic attitude towards one's writing.

The short serial is usually of five or six half-hour episodes, although some commercial radio companies now use episodes of ten or fifteen minutes. And there is evidence to suppose that these 'quickie' serials will become more and more popular in the future.

For the short radio serial, you will need all of the expertise and know-how that you would for a play, plus an understanding of what a radio serial aims to achieve. In a sense, each episode has to be capable of being satisfying radio for the person who is following it regularly, and also for the person who 'just happens' to be listening to that episode. This means that each episode has to, in some way, indicate what has gone before and extend that story. But you cannot recapitulate all of the story so far as may have been the habit in the past.

The first episode must establish some kind of situation with *significance* for the listener whose interest you wish to hold. As the Americans would say, it must promise a 'weeny', a prize for staying with the whole of the programme.

And the end of each episode except the last must have a 'hook' at the end. A question mark – what is going to happen next? The big trick with writing short serials is to be able to come up with interesting, unpredictable, yet rational hooks at the end of episodes. To some extent, if you can devise those hooks and a good ending for the last episode, the serial will almost write itself.

As we have already stated, you cannot recapitulate each episode after the first with an announcer explaining "What has happened so far – now listen on". That went out of fashion with the candle-snuffer. Nor can you use the last scene of the previous episode to start the next. What you have to do is to cheat a little. You take the last episode of the previous episode – condense it down to the barest possible minimum – then rewrite it as the first episode of the next episode.

Let us suppose that last episode had the hero and his girl trapped in a dungeon, with water rising rapidly up to their necks. The last words we heard were her's: – "Goodbye, Harry! I love you! I love you! Gurgle, gurgle, gurgle!" Fade out effects. Bring in theme music, fade down, announcer giving credits.

As it stands, that scene would be quite hopeless with which to begin your next episode. It would indicate that there is little hope for them (which is what you want the listener to believe) – then, bang, you have them out of trouble within a minute or two. It happens too quickly for there to be a build-up of suspense.

What you would do to start the next episode would be to start with your couple in water in the dungeon, but have the dialogue somewhat differently. Instead of the young lady gasping out her last despairing words of love, you could just have her struggling to remain afloat as the hero is working to get them out of their plight. Leave the scene with her saying that they only have a few minutes more in which to survive – then cut to an entirely different scene in order to hold the suspense – then return to the dungeon just in time for the hero to complete their safe delivery from danger.

Once again, we have used an example of purely thriller nature in order to make our point. But this is a technique which you can use for *any* type of serial.

We also said that it was the hero who was responsible for getting them out of danger, and not some outside agency. Whatever medium you write for – be it radio, TV, a novel, or anything else – you should be aware of the fact that it is far better for your hero or strongest character to work out his own salvation – it makes a much better human story.

For example: you are writing about a young widowed mother in a less socially conscious society in the past. She is poverty-stricken, has lost her employment and is about to be thrown into the cobbled street with her sickly babe. In order to have an interesting story, we have to see that young woman *in action*. We have to see her struggle to save her child, perhaps fail several times, and then emerge from her predicament largely by her own efforts. Even if it is only by the fact that she tears up her last petticoat with which to bind the wounds of a young man of means who then marries her.

If she were thrown into the street and then tripped over a bag containing one hundred gold sovereigns – you just don't have any story that is interesting enough to tell. And many, many would-be writers do, in fact, write this kind of story and expect it to sell. In a nutshell, you can say that the fortuitous coincidence or *total* outside assistance, offered freely without any strings are the very things which will kill a story stone dead. Either in high-key or low-key, there has to be effort invested in solving the story problem.

You may submit your radio serial in one of two forms. The first is to write a complete first episode, and attach the remaining episodes in the nature of 'thumb-nail sketches' of a page or two for each episode. This would be the method used by an experienced radio writer; particularly one who was on good terms with a radio producer who would be prepared to talk it over in detail. It is not to be recommended to the beginner.

After writing out that first episode in full, it can seem to be so clear how the remainder of the story will develop and how the scenes of each episode will be formed. However, as you would soon find out yourself, six half-hour episodes run for a total of three hours radio time, but require a lot more than the equivalent of three one-hour plays in the way of action, conflict, dramatic development and plot. This is because serials will use up material at a much faster pace than will the average play. You may thus find yourself embarrassed by the fact that, when you get down to the actual writing, you have run out of story by the end of episode four – or, sin of sins – you succumb to the temptation of putting in 'padding' to make up your time.

This does not mean that you cannot develop more plot and action to make up for the shortfall – of course you can. But, you may find that when you have done so, your whole serial is considerably different to one that you so confidently offered in the first place.

Consequently, the best course for the beginner is to write the whole serial out in full, so that when he submits it for consideration he knows that it is a completely workable proposition. If a rewrite should be called for, then he has a very secure framework which he can reshape. It takes considerable confidence in one's self to write out a piece as long as a radio serial purely as a speculative gamble. The writer must have something of the gambler in him, and be able to shrug off rejection lightly. It is certainly not for the writer who expects to win every time.

The best advice for the would-be writer of a radio serial, is to get a play or two accepted first, and get the confident assurance that one is now truly on the professional ladder. Then to grab the friendly ear of a producer and go over the proposition with him. Then that submission will, to some degree, have a welcome mat waiting for it.

# Chapter Five

## THE RADIO ADAPTATION

At first sight, adapting another person's work for radio may seem to be a plum job, with little to do but change a word or two here and there and to get it to the right length.

Certainly, most stage plays are relatively easy to adapt for broadcasting. But this is an area which is not readily open to the average freelance writer – particularly the beginner. You will find that most stage plays of any consequence have already been used – perhaps many, many times. Modern plays are often adapted by the original author, or by an established writer in the business who has the blessing of the original author. When you are experienced and well-known, adapting a stage play can be great fun, but no great attention should be given to it at the early stage of your career.

Books are sometimes adapted into one of three forms. The first is the *condensation* – often into fifteen minute episodes, and read out on the air by one person. A Book at Bedtime is such a programme. This treatment is more or less an editing job, and is often undertaken by an employee of the broadcasting company.

The second type of adaptation is to convert a book into a single play. Whether this can be done or not will, to a large extent, depend on the nature of the book itself. And that is about all that can be said about it. If it is possible to write a radio play of about twenty or thirty scenes which will do justice to the book and not reduce the story to an unacceptable skeleton – then that book can theoretically be adapted into a radio play.

The third kind of adaptation and the most often used, is the conversion of a book into a serial of perhaps five or six half-hour parts. You are then back to the ground which we have previously covered on the serial. It must tread a very tight storyline. There must be hooks at the end of the episodes. And, if there is an overall story mystery – then this must be concealed until the very last moment of the last episode.

If the original author has not written his book in this way (and many of them don't) then it is the responsibility of the radio scriptwriter to do so. And he is morally obliged to make any changes in such a manner that he remains true to the spirit of the original work. The best way to describe this is to say that the scriptwriter aims to write a radio version in the same way that the original writer would have done, had he been writing the story for radio.

Novelists are free to use as many story characters as they choose, as story characters cost nothing. The only limitation on numbers is if the reader is able to cope with them. The Victorian novelists did not have our modern attitude of writing for easy reading, and were prone to use many, many characters in their stories. Even a modern novel can have twenty or so characters, all of whom play an essential and specialised role in the story.

This is the largest problem which faces the scriptwriter. There would not be twenty actors available to him in the studio at the recording of each episode. He has to group the episodes so that he only uses six to eight actors in each or he must refashion the story so that fewer characters are needed to carry out the actions and motivations required by the story. This doesn't mean that he can leave out any action because he cannot afford to use the character. He just gives each character more work to do.

Supposing the hero is being badgered by three rather nasty people. Tom keeps him awake at night with a blaring record-player. Dick steals his milk. And Harry spreads untrue gossip about him. In order to reduce characters for the radio version, the scriptwriter can choose one of these characters as the most likely villain – be it Tom, Dick or Harry – say Harry. Then Harry makes the hero's life hell by keeping him awake until the early hours – takes his milk – and spreads lies about him. It sometimes can be quite a puzzle to work this one out – without writing an entirely different story!

The biggest mistake that you could ever make in adapting a book into a serial is to start work on it without checking one or two important questions.

The copyright of a work belongs to the original author for the rest of his life, and then to his successors for a period of fifty years from the date of his death. During that period of time, it is illegal for anyone to use that material in any form without permission. The Russians will, but this book deals with scriptwriting, and not ungentlemanly behaviour!

So, you see, you may not adapt the work of a living author, or one who has been dead for less than fifty years, without permission. If you know the publisher of the last edition of the book, you can contact them, and through them, the author or the author's literary agent. You should not be at all surprised to be told that permission cannot be granted to you – as the radio rights may have already been granted to another party, or incorporated in a film contract which includes radio and TV. You just have to accept it as a fact of life and go in search of another book.

If you are told that these rights have not yet been disposed of, then you should check on the interest of the radio company in your proposal to submit a serial. It could be that they would just not be interested. They may already have a considerable number of serials 'in-the-can' or planned for the next year or so. Or, the book that you are proposing to serialise may be too similar to another which they have in mind. *And*, it is only honest to say this – if you are about to write your first script – they may not want to find that you send them something which is quite awful, and then be accused of over-encouraging you.

As we said earlier on, there are some areas of scriptwriting which are best left until you have proved your ability and you are known to one or two people. By that time, it could well be that you will be invited to take on an adaptation. The best advice that could be given to you is, if you know of a good book which you would like to adapt – make a note of it – and keep it a dark secret until you can put it to good use. And just hope that nobody beats you to it!

# Chapter Six

## THE RADIO DOCUMENTARY

This is usually an area which offers very few opportunities for the freelance writer – particularly if he has not yet earned himself a reputation.

The reason is very easy to understand if you take account of the aims and purposes of a radio documentary unit. To some extent, it is tied to the current affairs policy of the broadcasting company. It is not bound to use only topical material, but the emphasis tends to be on what is happening now – what may soon be in the public area of interest, and the marking of anniversaries. As such, the documentary unit cannot just wait for material 'to turn up'. It must either plan ahead to ensure that it has what it needs, or have on call those people who are capable of providing material very quickly. So, much of this work is done either by staff or known freelances with their own specialities.

However, that does not completely exclude any chance of selling them a good idea.

Radio companies around the world work in many different ways. We have the very professional and excellent BBC in Britain – in the opinion of many the best radio organization in the world. Depending on finance and other factors, the size and expertise of other companies then dwindles down to almost one man with a microphone, a playing deck and a transmitter. So it is not possible to describe a working pattern that all radio companies use. But we can describe, in round terms how the BBC operates.

It has a documentary unit, which we have mentioned above.

It also has a drama unit which, although not a law unto itself, is free to select and produce plays on a regular basis which it aims to be suitable for each of the BBC networks. You could say that so long as it keeps each of these networks happy, then it can use its own power of choice. And, presumably, there would soon be a complaint from the networks if they felt that they were not being properly served!

Another interesting unit is the Radio Light Entertainment Department. The working arrangement here is slightly different to the Drama Department. It is usual for Light Entertainment to go through the ideas offered to them, and then to check them out with the most suitable of the BBC Networks. If they get an approval, then they will go ahead and make the programme or, if it is a series or serial, they may make a pilot episode first.

This working arrangement is not completely clear-cut, but that describes it in the most general terms.

Under the heading of Light Entertainment comes Comedy in all its forms. There are also Serials, both light and dramatic. The Light Entertainment Department also makes those programmes which are of a near-documentary nature, but not so documentary as to fall exclusively into the province of the Radio Documentary Unit.

And it is with this kind of documentary that the newly-established scriptwriter may be able to score. The point is, do we call it a documentary, or do we call it a general light entertainment programme? For our purposes, we could say that if the programme is based on factual figures, places and events, then we can treat it as mainly documentary.

The treatment of this kind of material could be quite serious or very light. It could deal with the establishment of the Thames River Police or 'The Man Who Collects Famous False Teeth'.

It could be told by a narrator, with or without interviews. It could be told wholly or partly through dialogue, just as is done with a dramatic work.

It could include music, with or without the above-mentioned aspects. But it would not be a purely musical programme of a middle-to-upper-crust nature, as this would be produced by the quite separate Music Department.

So you will appreciate that it can take more than just good scriptwriting in order to be at home in the radio world. One needs to understand how the machinery works. This book gives you the bulk of that information.

If this light-entertainment kind of documentary is the type of script that you aim to write, then you should start by listening to as many as you can to get the 'feel' of the kind of material which is used. You will probably find that some of the programmes you hear are not the kind which you would wish to write, whilst others will immediately appeal to you. Make a brief note of each subject and the way in which it was handled.

You will probably find that those which appealed to you most were the work of one or two particular producers. So make a note of their names as well.

It would be entirely untrue to say that any producer will only turn out one kind of programme – the evidence is all against that charge – at least with the BBC Radio Light Entertainment Department. These producers, since the beginning of time, have shown how adaptable and versatile they can be. Nevertheless, just as you, the writer, will put your own personal stamp on the work that you write, so a producer will have his own favoured avenues which he would like to explore – even if he doesn't realise it until he sees your proposal.

Having to some extent mapped out an area or areas which would seem to be very much to your fancy, you should then write up your proposal and send it to the producer who would seem to be your best bet. You may not hit the target first time, but if your idea and your presentation are good, then it makes an excellent 'calling-card'.

Sometimes it takes a little time and sweat to break into new writing areas. Any good script which is well received but rejected does your name *some* good in the long term. And, as we have mentioned before, just because an idea is rejected at the present moment does not mean that it has breathed its last and must now be buried or cremated. Keep it safely, because in a year or so from now it could be quite differently received. You also have to consider the possibilities of MILKING AN IDEA DRY, a subject which we will look at later on in this book.

Any socially responsible radio company will try to cater for minority tastes where it can – but the main emphasis is on the most popular appeal. Remember that when you choose your subject. Aim for the taste of the largest possible radio audience.

# *Chapter Seven*

## RADIO COMEDY

There are basically two areas of radio comedy. And the first of these we can cover very quickly. It is the 'stand-up' comedy or gag show which is a direct descendant of the Victorian/Edwardian music-hall turn. There are now sophisticated variations on these original single and double acts, which carry a variety of modern descriptions such as 'sequential entertainment' – 'road shows' – 'The Joe Bloggs Show' – and 'Topical New Looks At Life'. Some are supported by musical items. Their content varies considerably from show to show. There are sketches, 'quickies', black-outs, one-liners, 'news headlines', 'a-funny-thing-happened-to-me' monologues, 'cod impersonations' and club-type routines. They are nearly all designed to get the fast and loud laugh – and that is the only test of their effectiveness and success.

To some extent, you have to have been born with more than your fair share of funny-bone in order to do well as a gag-writer. But the art can be developed or learned. The biggest factor which you can have going for you is to live or work in the company of those who will 'josh' with you; where your day gets at least some witty conversation and cross-fire – to challenge and sharpen your ability to come back with something to top the other person's wise-crack. You do not have to go around wearing a red nose and grinning until your face aches, just keep yourself in stimulating company – and try to keep your distance from the Misery Merchants. You may not get to be the world's top gagwriter – but you will find life more enjoyable.

If gagwriting is what you want to do, then listen to existing shows. They will most probably have already been recorded and completed by the time you hear them. But you can always write a short and polite letter to the producer asking if any more are planned and, if so, would he let you know when, so that you can submit some material. You could also write a few pieces for him showing what you would have submitted to the programme which you have just heard, by way of showing what you are capable of doing. You will surely receive a courteous reply and perhaps even be offered an opportunity to submit something for another show which is being planned. Remember one thing. It is better to submit a few excellent items than many that are trite and dated.

The second area of radio humour is the situation-comedy. And if there is anywhere in writing for radio where it is possible to get it all wrong and make a right mess of it, it is here.

In the first place, a situation-comedy is nowhere near to being a comedy play – which is an entirely different animal altogether – and the fact cannot be emphasized too strongly. All too many scripts which are submitted as pretending to be situation comedies are, in fact, farces. Farces can be fine when kept where they belong. They rarely, if ever, belong in radio situation comedy.

What do we mean by farce? The Oxford dictionary describes it as: – 'Dramatic piece meant merely to excite laughter; this branch of drama; absurdly futile proceedings.' This is a good description, but it does not serve our present need for *absolute* accuracy, because it also describes very well the meaning of situation-comedy and, as we have already, there *is* a difference.

It is better to describe the word farce in purely theatrical (or radio and TV) terms. A farce is a play with unreal characters in unreal situations. Or, if you prefer, ridiculous characters in ridiculous situations.

Farces can come across well on the stage. A few have been successful on radio and even less on TV. But they do tend to be the one-off piece. And the few situation comedies with some farcical leanings which have been produced on radio and TV have been the result of very considerable accomplishments from all of the artists and studio staff involved.

Put simply: your guideline for situation comedy is to have real people in unreal situations. Or the opposite; unreal people in real situations. Try mixing the two factors and you will get something which is 'silly'. Too silly even to be funny, usually.

Just recall a few of the funniest radio or TV *series* known to you. Write them down. Cross out that great classic THE GOON SHOW. How many farces are there? You can probably count them on the fingers of one foot!

It is most important that a proposal for a situation comedy

should have plenty of 'mileage' – the situation and the characters should have the potential for many, many stories. That doesn't quite mean that either you or the radio company would hope or expect that the series should run for evermore – although some have nearly done so. But there should be a *choice* of a great number of plots – and the more that there potentially are – the more chance you have of scooping off the very best as you would the cream off the milk.

It is not the purpose of this book to discourage you from trying anything you want in whatever way you want. Our very best writers are nearly all individualists, who consistently break the rules laid down by other people and thereby break new and interesting ground. So, if you have an idea which convinces you that it would make a terrific situation comedy series, then go ahead and have a shot at it.

But, just think over what I've said about preferably only working on material which has 'mileage'. You need a basic situation which has many permutations, wherever possible *using the same characters in each episode*. And this is a significance which many would-be sit-com writers do not understand.

Let us say, for example, that the situation which you have in mind is that of a second-hand car business. Bearing in mind what we have already said about keeping most of your characters throughout all the episodes – you would have, say, the 'Guvner' and his office girl, the slick and almost criminal salesman, and perhaps the mechanic who doesn't really know his bumper from his elbow-wrench.

With a basic team such as this, you could construct your stories so that, although the characters are selling second-hand cars, there would also be room for comedy interplay which did not use the second-hand car aspect – namely, the more personal stories.

If – alternatively – you took the line of concentrating on selling a second-hand car to someone in each episode, then there would be a considerable similarity in each of the episodes, and the people in the business would hardly come alive. The determining factor is not the *situation*, but how you treat it.

An established radio writer would present this idea in this fashion – three or four pages describing the situation and its regular characters, plus their relationship to one and other. Then there would be one completely written episode, and five or twelve episode outlines – or 'thumbnails' as they are called. He would submit five or twelve, depending on whether the series was intended to run for six or thirteen episodes. That is what an established professional would do, and a newcomer could certainly do no less.

In fact, a newcomer should put in perhaps three or four completed episodes, if only to prove that he was something more than just a 'one-script writer'.

# *Chapter Eight*

## THE RADIO TALK

By its own definition, the radio talk is more talk than writing. But the talk must first be written so that it may be considered and perhaps adapted. And the talk is always written by the person who is going to deliver it. If he speaks it and didn't write it, then it isn't a talk – it is the narration of another kind of material.

So, if you want to give a talk on radio – just write it up and send it in. Get your guidelines by listening to talks put out by the radio company whom you hope to interest. Get an idea of the *scope* of the subjects used. And, what is most important, make a note of the running time – and fix your own length accordingly.

Back in the section on the Radio Short Story, we said that fifteen minutes of story would need about 2,150 words. Use that measurement to gauge the number of words that you will need for your talk.

# *Chapter Nine*

## RADIO FOR CHILDREN

Referring again to an earlier part of this book, it was said that many novice writers assumed that they should start at the bottom by writing the half-hour play first, then building up the length as they became more skilled. We get precisely the same attitude when a person decides to start by using his limited abilities to write for children, and then work up the age groups as he becomes more competent.

This could only be a valid course of action in the very smallest area of radio-writing for children. You have to remember that you may be writing for very young children, but it isn't the children who buy your script!

The very easiest way in would be to write an eight-hundred-word short story for the tiny tots – that is, if there is a demand for them. This you would have to check by listening to your local and national radio. If they don't seem to be using them, then don't bother to send any in for the time being. Much of children's radio follows a very set pattern which may be slow to change. So, if they are not using this kind of short stories, then it is highly possible that they definitely would not be interested.

For most of the other kind of material used for children's programmes – check back to the relevant sections in this book and shape your writing accordingly. Just make sure that you treat your juvenile audience with the dignity that they deserve and don't write down at the 'cootchy-coo' level.

One particular area which is well worth considering is writing for schools programmes. One does not need to be a qualified teacher or have a degree in any particular subject in order to do this. You are not teaching – you are writing a radio script.

The programme producers will often put over an idea of a social nature in a dramatised form. 'George Falls Foul Of The Law' – 'Mary Looks For Her First Job' – 'Joe Wants To Be A Doctor'. These subjects are often presented almost as a radio play. If this is what you would like to do – then just write to The Head of Schools Programmes of your radio company – sending along an example of your writing at the same time. There is often an opening that you may be able to fill.

Sad to say, the payment is usually quite poor – so there may not be too many writers kicking down the doors for work in this area. If you can strike up an interest in yourself, then you will probably be given the basic material to dramatise, or be pointed in the direction where you can get it for yourself. And although the pay is not of the highest, you could well find that the characters in your story are played by quite famous actors who give some of their working time in this way as a public service. Wouldn't *that* be something to make your neighbours jealous!

# Chapter Ten

## MAKING A START IN RADIO

We must not try and pretend that you have been told all that there is to learn about radio scriptwriting in these few pages. Let us say that you now have about half of what it takes.

You will be delighted to know that you can get the other half just by putting your feet up and closing your eyes, and *listening* to radio. But don't make too much of a rest of it. Listening with a very critical ear can be quite hard work.

If, for example, you are going to study a play by listening to it, then you should read quickly through that part of this book and make some notes of what you are going to pay particular attention to. How long are the scenes on average? How did the play start? How do you see the actors grouped in the studio? How are the effects used?

All these questions and more should be asked. And what did you think of the play *as a play*? Do you feel as though you had partaken of a tasty and satisfying meal? Or do you feel that there was something lacking? Did it give you pleasant dramatic surprises? Or was it all pretty predictable and had you yawning before the end?

Now that you have a yardstick with which to measure that kind of programme, you will find that your knowledge of writing for radio will increase by leaps and bounds each time you listen in.

And now for the bad news! Once you have accustomed yourself to listening with an informed and critical ear – you will never again be able to go back to the days when, virgin-like, you listened to the radio with reverence. Instead, you will tend to become a fairly difficult fellow to please. Your standards will be much higher, and you will often say to yourself: – "The writer really wasted a good opportunity in that scene. If it had been me, I would have ..."

Of course, you will sometimes get quite the reverse effect, and get pleasure from the fact that you understand precisely how the writer combined artistry with good radio technique to achieve something which was unbelievable good. And, if you are wise, you will start itching to do it for yourself.

# II

# *Writing for Television*

# Chapter Eleven

## AN INTRODUCTION TO TV SCRIPTWRITING

When this book first came into your hands, you may posibly have thought that about half of the pages would deal with radio, and the other half with TV. But as we said earlier on, the main emphasis has been placed on radio writing.

The advantage of this arrangement is that there now isn't a lot of information to give you concerning TV scriptwriting, because most of the basic essentials have already been covered. We now only have to deal with the finer points concerning the audio-visual medium of the box.

With radio, you are writing for the ear, and the ear alone. So it could now seem that all you have to do is to add the visual part and you will have a fine TV script. Totally wrong. You can be absolutely certain that if actors took a radio script and acted it out in front of the cameras using the body movements and gestures that the dialogue seemed to demand you would have something pretty awful on your hands. It would seem embarrassingly 'stagey' and wordy.

Now why should a fine radio play come across in that fashion when it is visually acted out?

The answer is that in your radio script, you have subtly inserted in the dialogue those clues from which the listener can build his own visual pictures. Mary says to Bill, "Here – a nice cup of tea." And the listener 'sees' the cup of char pass from Mary to Bill.

In the TV version of this action, we actually see the passing of the cup. For Mary to then say, "Here – a nice cup of tea", is stating the obvious. It is just as superfluous as seeing a young man with a beaming smile across his face, and he says to us, "You may not have guessed it, but I am very happy." We *know* he is happy – he doesn't need to tell us. Does he think we are blind?

You will remember the golden rule which was mentioned early on in this book when we said that every word should have a purpose. It should:

MOVE THE STORY FORWARD
REVEAL CHARACTER
CREATE ATMOSPHERE
CAUSE A LAUGH

In our TV script, when Mary says to Bill, "Here – a nice cup of tea," her words do none of these things. She doesn't move the story forward, nor reveal character, nor create any atmosphere. And if she gets any sort of laugh, then it will probably be one that you neither wished for or intended. Can you see the difference between the radio and TV approach in this example? Once you have thoroughly understood it, then you will automatically use the right treatment for the right kind of script.

Rather than waste the words, we have Mary say something which would satisfy one or more of the above-mentioned conditions. She could say: "Here, you deserve this," that would build a little character for us. Alternatively, she could give the cup to Bill and say, "Here – I hope it chokes you." Again, that builds character, creates some atmosphere, *and* moves the story forward because Bill is now obliged to make some reaction to those hard words. *And*, in certain kinds of story, it may even get a laugh.

You would be well advised to spend a little time carrying out some experiments in this area. Think up a line of dialogue for radio which is intended to 'show' action. Then use this line for a TV script and actually show the action visually. Finally, produce a different line of dialogue which *really adds something to the story.*

As we can actually see the TV version of your play, we can use a few little tricks which are not available to you on radio – tricks which you should get into the habit of using.

For example, one scene of your radio play may run for a nice average of three minutes which, for radio, is not too long to become boring. In this scene, Madge is telling her friend that husband Bernard is working late at the office. We have to wait until this scene is finished before we can play the scene of Bernard 'working' by taking an attractive secretary into a restaurant. There is nothing wrong with telling the story this way on radio – it could probably come across very well.

But move that scene over to TV and it could drag its feet. What you can do is to slip in a short piece of Bernard entering the restaurant whilst Madge is talking to her friend – perhaps with her voice continuing over this little snippet. Or, the friend could be nodding her head in agreement, and we hear her 'think', "I've heard *that* one before!"

We mentioned earlier on how listening to a person's thoughts on radio can give a feeling of unreality. But strangely enough, you can sometimes get away with it on TV. Perhaps it does not seem to be at all unreasonable to the viewer because his eye is taking in some quite normal behaviour visually.

We also mentioned that radio had the best scenery in the world. You are able to move freely from cellar to attic – from Delhi to Glasgow. You do not have this freedom with TV. If all or part of the play is taken on location (which means anything that is not a studio set) then it can be used to its fullest extent, but even that can be limited compared with the possibilities of radio.

No TV company expects to be able to perform every play in one room built in the studio. That would appear to be far too 'stagey'. Although it is sometimes done, not for economy, but to project that stage-like quality. The TV company will build sufficient sets in which to perform the play, but you have to remember that building the sets for the inside of a semi-detached can often cost nearly as much as actually building a real house!

You, the writer, have to be able to strike a reasonable balance with costs, and this will reflect itself in the way you present your story. A good tip would be – never use any set only once.

You should also strive for economy with your words.

Sometimes a character can 'speak' by just a gesture of the hand, by a shrug, by a grimace. And this could be far more effective than the words which you would use on radio. You can also employ the technique of having an actor playing against his lines. He is asked how he is enjoying his glass of dandelion wine. "It's fantastic!" he says. But his screwed-up mouth tells us otherwise.

Your TV dialogue should be tighter – shorter – and never duplicate what we are seeing. Having said that, it is only fair to caution you against going too far in that direction, to the point where the actors are speaking in monosyllables. That old-time Western film star, Gary Cooper, built a reputation in just saying, "Yup!" Watch one of his old movies if you get the chance. The rest of the cast had to make up his short-fall of words, or we would never have known what the devil the story was all about. Use good judgement in how much dialogue you use.

Somewhere in this book we should say something about sex and violence, so it may as well be here. You do see S & V on TV, let's admit it. Some people are for it – some are against. What stand should you take? A little piece of information may help you to make up your mind.

TV companies receive many, many uninvited scripts each week. Most will be from novice writers. And some would seem to come from very sick people indeed. If you care to put down a list of all the depravities you can dream up, you will probably not have included all of those that are included in scripts submitted in any year.

If nature has left us with sufficient of the right hormones, then we are quite capable of engaging in some slap-and-tickle. If only some of these scripts would only be satisfied with that! For, try as one may, if it is a dud story, then all the bare bottoms and bloody noses in the world are not going to make it the tiniest degree better. If you want to be a dirty old man in your script-writing, then work up to it slowly until you discover how far you are permitted to go.

# *Chapter Twelve*

## TV COMEDY

We have already covered the basic ground of comedy writing in the radio section, and shown some differences between the treatments of scripts.

The biggest problem which we come up against in writing for TV comedy shows is that each of us has his own particular idea of what constitutes comedy. There is something of a paradox here which is worth a brief mention. A group of would-be TV comedy writers could sit and watch a programme together and all agree that the programme was very funny and enjoyable. There seems to be this common ground where watching and listening are concerned. But if each of these neophytes were then to attempt to write a comedy script of their own devising, the results would be varied and, mainly, quite unfunny.

In the eyes of the writer, his script would seem to be up to production standard, but quite often it does not make much of an impression on anyone else. There could be many answers to this vexing puzzle. It could possibly be that the script just isn't funny anyway. And we can all tend to feel that our baby is the most beautiful one in the world. Thus a clue to why many, many scripts are just not found to be funny may be in this area of loving one's own child.

To a large extent, when we write dramatic material, we are pursuing the path of our own concocted plot-line and bringing out our own particular sympathies and antipathies towards real people, times, situations and places. And providing that there is an eventual sense of wholeness, rationality and story, then we are at liberty to go through the ups and downs of human emotions as we please. It is very much like shaking ice cubes in a bucket – shake them about for long enough, and most of them will settle down face-to-face and make a virtual whole.

When we write comedy, the freedoms and liberties which are open to us are of a far different kind. From the first line until the last, we carry the unavoidable obligation to be funny – and nothing but funny.

Let us suppose that we have just finished writing a quite good TV comedy script. In fact, it is so good that it has an average of six laughs per page – which is not top-flight comedy – but getting close to it. Our script then gets through to the TV studio floor. Most of our laugh-lines work out very well in perfomance. In fact, a couple turn out to be far funnier than even we would have expected. But one or two on each page do not do quite as well as we had hoped. They are still funny but, if we are honest, they are only worth a slight titter or smile.

The programme is then broadcast. We sit with a group of viewers and find that some of our funnies strike a response from everyone present – say a third – then those which we knew to be flat make very little impression, although there may be some residual response from the good stuff which went before. The remaining third of our lines gets a varied reaction – some people obviously think that they are funny – others do not.

Looked at in this way, you will understand that you cannot assume that everything which you wrote to get a laugh is going to work. Let us be really brutal, and say that you are only going to have a fifty percent success.

So how do you write a TV comedy script which is going to be successful? You allow for this unavoidable wastage by being twice as funny as you need to be. And that is what TV comedy script-writing is all about – your material has to be funny in quality and quantity. Like the farmer who ensures that he will raise sufficient wheat for his needs, you plant far more than you need. Then let the birds come and raid the field, let there be cold spells and dry spells, let nasty wriggly things in the ground do their worst and picnickers sit on what they will – there will still be plenty over.

Have you ever watched a comedy show and, afterwards, said to yourself, "I didn't think *that* was funny"? Well, in script form it probably was. The writer just didn't put in enough to compensate for what was lost on its way through the production system.

One could write a book about what constitutes humour, in fact many books have been written. Is there one short, crisp and golden rule which we could formulate here? Let us try.

If you were to hold a book a few inches away from your nose

then, during the period of fifteen seconds you were to bring it slowly into contact with yourself and press your nose flat – that action would have little effect that could be noticed. Now reduce the speed to a quarter of a second, and you will most probably suffer a nose-bleed.

Drink a bottle of strong Devon cider over the course of a week. And then drink a similar bottle in one hour.

Whether you now have a broken nose, or you are too drunk to care – you have experienced an *impact*. Something collided with you – quite unexpected – BOP! Once too often, a man insults a waitress on a personal level. She dumps the plate of soup straight into his lap – splosh! She didn't warn him. He didn't see it coming. The first he knew of it was the impact.

Of course, we can derive pleasure from many things which carry no impact. Puppies tumbling in the grass – toddlers dressed in grown-up clothes – the Greek soldier in ceremonial dress, complete with a ballerina skirt and pom-poms on his slippers. They make us smile. We find them amusing. But just let that Greek soldier have his skirt drop suddenly to his ankles and we have impact. We have the quite unexpected – we have comedy.

Now, supposing we notice well in advance that the soldier's tu-tu is separating from his bodice. We see the gap slowly yawning – his string vest showing through the widening gap. We find that funny, yet the impact has not occurred for the moment. That is anticipation. And what are we anticipating? That precise and delicious moment when the last strand of thread gives up the ghost and – impact.

Or suppose that the soldier became aware of the impending disaster and held onto his frilly skirt with both hands. You still enjoyed the anticipation, didn't you? The anticipation of an impact, which may have occurred. So one golden rule we can bear in mind when writing comedy for TV is that we aim to get impact or threats of impact.

That rule will cover most of the whole comedy writing field. Sketches, one-liners, gags and situation comedies – they all depend to some extent on impact – hard – fast – now. Not gentle – slow – and next week. If you are not trying to reveal character, advance a story line, or create atmosphere – then you must be concentrating solely on getting a laugh. No wasted words – not even one. And don't wait for the laughter to die down, go straight into your next funny as quick as you can, and let the comedian or actor worry about the pace of delivery.

We can slip another small rule in here. If your audience has time to think between each laugh, then you are wasting time and words. You don't want your audience to think – you want them to respond.

You deliver an impact, they respond – then another impact, and so on. This may seem to be far too mechanical to those who consider writing to be a high form of art. Don't you believe it! The skill here is in employing an economy of words – of aiming for an effect and achieving it every time. The ability to do that requires a much higher standard of writing than some other areas do – which is supported by the fact that comedy scriptwriters receive much higher rates of pay for their work; sometimes earning far more than a Prime Minister.

With situation comedy – the acted piece, as opposed to the performed piece, we have another factor which helps us to turn out a good script. It is the factor of disagreement.

Any comic situation contains some element of disagreement. The incident concerning the Greek soldier is only funny because he was (or would be) in disagreement with the proposition of being seen in his underpants. If he chose to let his skirt fall, we should not find that at all funny. Depending on how we look at life, we should find him to be objectionable, pitiable, or downright boring.

To some extent, we are again back in the realm of dramatic writing – the other side of the same coin. The coin of disagreement can be spent in any area of fiction, and is one that you should be in the habit of carrying in your pocket, because you will always find that you have a need for it.

Disagreement with what? That is a very large question indeed. Joe disagrees with Bill, crooks disagree with the law, Egyptian tap water disagrees with Western tummies. There seems to be so much potential disagreement about that it is difficult to know where to start. It would be difficult to pin down unless we were to confine it to one side of the disagreeing pair of items. It becomes much more understandable if we reduce the instances above to Joe or the crooks or a Western tummy.

Let us see if we can develop this proposition into a list which covers all possible kinds of disagreement. Since the earliest of recorded times, philosophers have said that Man has only three activities in which he can engage. He can BE. He can DO. And he can HAVE. They didn't give all the possibilities, because there is a negative side to that claim. A man can NOT be. He can NOT do. And he can NOT have. So, how can we use this to cover the whole gamut of possible disagreements?

Let us choose one person and call him Joe. We will write down all the situations in which Joe can find himself based on what the philosophers have taught us.

1. Joe can be something.
2. Joe can do something.
3. Joe can have something.

Well, three cheers for Joe. He is having a nice uneventful life. And we only wish that ours was as uneventful.

4. Joe can not be something.
5. Joe can not do something.
6. Joe can not have something.

Joe has now become Mr Average, because there are some of these aspects in everybody's life. For instance, he cannot be the President of the United States, cannot do a sword-swallowing act, or have ten wives all at the same time. He may disagree with these things which his life lacks, but his disagreement is hardly of the kind which we need for comedy or drama.

Now let us take this list of six items and have Joe disagree with them. We shall reword each example so that it makes sense.

7. Joe wants to be something, but can't.
8. Joe wants to do something, but can't.
9. Joe wants to have something, but can't.
10. Joe doesn't want to be something, but must.
11. Joe doesn't want to do something, but must.
12. Joe doesn't want to have something, but must.

We can add to this Joe's broad disagreement with things which are going on at a distance which are not so much his own concern. His son has his head shaved, and Joe believes this to be all wrong. His disagreement is actually number nine on our list. Joe wants to have a son with a head of hair, but can't.

If, instead, Joe objects because the son of a neighbour has his head shaved, then finding Joe's position on our list becomes somewhat woolly, and we shall just have to say he is a nosey-parker or inclined to be a person who disagrees with everything with which he doesn't happen to agree.

In your comedy and dramatic writing, this kind of person who objects to everything on principle can often play some part, but it is really a type of character we are discussing and not the more important kinds of disagreement which makes meaty situations for you to write about.

So, if you aim to write situation comedy for TV, stay with the elements of four to twelve which we have listed above. Have impacts, or threats of impacts. Don't waste a word, and put in more potential laughs to allow for those which don't eventually make it. And use all of the pointers which were brought to your notice in the section dealing with TV Drama.

Also bear in mind that the basic elements of characterisation that were covered in radio still apply with TV. In general terms, you are looking for unbelievable characters in believable situations, and believable characters in unbelievable situations. You will want to avoid farce like the plague, but it is possible to use believable characters in believable situations. When you do this, then you need to be a really superb comedy writer, and just as adept with handling drama.

# *Chapter Thirteen*

## WRITING FOR TELEVISION GENERALLY

In the two sections of this book which deal with television comedy and drama, we have shown that they are both extensions and developments of the radio forms. So it is in the other areas of television such as documentaries, features, serials, adaptations and children's programmes. The very best way to learn how to do it, once you have the basic rules and know what to look for, is to watch those programmes for which you wish to write.

This book encourages you to try your hand at any form of programme. There are two reasons for this encouragement. The first is for you to gain experience and flexibility in the way that you express your ideas and to get to feel 'at home' in radio and television. In this changing world in which we live, adaptability and diversification are being demanded of us more and more. Radio and television are also part of this changing world.

We have mentioned before that a good script can be rejected for the sole reason that the script larder is full to capacity., For example, at the time when these words were written, one major television company had forty-five documentaries 'in the can' – all waiting to be found slots in the broadcasting schedule; all of them completely finished and just waiting for screening.

A great deal of investment was tied up here, and there would be little economic logic in churning out many more for the moment. The result of this stockpiling is that the TV company in question is looking at any new proposals with a more than critical eye. It is a buyer's market (more so than usual) and only the very best ideas stand a chance of being accepted.

Of course, other companies may not be in this position; some of them may be crying out for documentary ideas. But you see how it is possible for markets to fluctuate.

We mentioned before that a good idea is a good idea, and what is not accepted now should be put to one side for submission later. However, there is a limit to how far you would want to keep on writing for a future and unspecified date. You should make sure that you have the capability of writing for more than one kind of programme. In other words, you become an opportunist. The market for radio and television scripts does not diminish – it only changes. All you have to do, is change with it.

The second reason why you should flex your writing arm in more than one direction is one which is very understandable to most professional and successful scriptwriters. In fact, it is understood by experienced writers in any field.

It is the 'when-I-grow-up' syndrome which we see in its most obvious manifestation with little boys who express their burning desire to be a train-driver, or a fireman, or to follow some other such occupation. Very few little boys ever do actually become train-drivers or firemen, but is is an interesting fact, that most of these little boys eventually find careers which are in the broad categories where train-drivers or firemen are to be found.

The would-be train-driver may never have any actual connection with the railways, but he could well find himself a niche where he is in some way involved with travel or transportation. This could be anything from a bus-driver, to a travel agent, to an aircraft designer. His intelligence, aptitude, circumstances, opportunities and inclination will eventually tend to finalise the result in due course.

In other words, there was something inside the little boy, some intuition, dream, hope – call it what you will – which indicated to him some vague area where he knew he could fit in and be happy. Only experience and opportunity prevent him from being more precise about where he wants to go in his later years. When concrete experience is actually available to him, and he has good reason to suppose that opportunity will also be available, then he quite commonly states with unerring accuracy what he wants to grow up to be. If the child of a doctor, a musician, dentist, artist, craftsman – any well defined profession – if this child states at an early age that he wishes to tread in the footsteps of the parent – then you could safely lay money on the probability of him doing exactly that.

But what has all of this to do with we writers?

Well, when we are 'little boys' in this writing game – when we first feel this urge to put our thoughts to paper – we also experience the 'when-I-grow-up' phase.

We could say, "Ah! (when I grow up) – I want to write plays

which will make people look at themselves and behave better." Or, "No, (when I grow up) – I want to write a best-selling novel."

Of course, some writers do start with so firm an intention and eventually achieve that aim. But, when they are completely honest, most writers will admit to the fact that they are a little surprised to find that their best writing successes are quite different to what they dreamed of at the beginning of their writing careers. There is no shame in making these admissions. Writing is an educative process. The more you write the more you learn about writing, communicating, how you feel about things, perhaps about the world in general, and perhaps about yourself. And, if every time you sit down to write you aim to do your best, this education tends to be quite fast.

Once you actually begin to write in earnest, you will find your horizons opening up. Half way through your serious radio play, you could well feel that you would like to follow it with something of a lighter nature – or perhaps a humorous novel. These things do happen. But that would be no good excuse for you to drop your radio play half-finished and, like Stephen Leacock's Duchess, leap onto your horse and go dashing off in all directions at the same time.

You always owe yourself the obligation of trying to complete everything you start. And, in passing, we must also mention that many, many of the finest pieces of writing have known moments – and even weeks – when the author believed that any further progress was quite impossible. You always owe yourself the dedication to finish what you've started.

The important point which we are trying to convey here is that you may start with the strong desire to write, and that in itself is a very good indicator that success of some sort awaits you somewhere in the future. But experience – the experience which you get from actually developing your writing skills – will almost certainly change your original plans for what you want to write most.

Add to this the opportunities which will surely come your way if you are active and productive and look for them, and then add the other possibilities which life in general serves up to all of us. You may well find that there is an unsuspected branch of scriptwriting which is very much your *metier*. If you try your hand at nearly everything, you too could get a pleasant surprise.

# III

# *Making the Most of Yourself*

# *Chapter Fourteen*

## MILKING AN IDEA DRY

If there is any one single tip in this book which should be printed in capital letters, *and* red ink, *and* underlined *and* presented on a silver platter, this is it.

Milking an idea dry has a very obvious and self-evident meaning. You take one idea, and get every treatment, every development and every piece of writing out of it which you can.

Let us take treatment first. You have an idea for a radio play and write it up. Perhaps you sell this radio play, or perhaps you don't. Either way, you should eventually do your best to get a TV play out of it. You will find that when you write the TV version that the story and the characters are now more convincing and stronger. And that would only be to be expected, since you cannot help but add something to your material every time you work it. Once again, perhaps your TV treatment will be accepted and perhaps it will not. There is now the possibility of a stage play, a short story – or even a novel. This is basically what we mean by milking an idea dry.

There is also an extension to this principle which should concern you if you are interested in the subject of money – and that is milking a *script* dry, as opposed to milking the *idea* dry.

We will suppose that you have written a good radio play. You had the BBC in mind for the submission. If the BBC buys it, then it has the rights on the English version for a year or so. The English rights then revert back to you. The foreign rights are yours to do with as you wish at any time.

Or, the BBC returns the script to you with thanks, but no thank you. Whatever happens, you know that you have a good radio play which you wish to offer to other parts of the world – English-speaking or not.

If the play really is good, then you may be able to sell it many times over – *but only if it appeals to the overseas companies*. That is what you have to bear in mind. A play which was designed solely to appeal to the most insular tastes of British listeners, to be so aimed at a purely national audience – could possibly be of small interest to overseas – who have their own insular tastes and national interests. In order to succeed with a world-wide success of sales, you must start with an international idea before you write the play.

What this means, in effect, is that if you are aiming for world sales then you use only those story ideas and treatments which give you the best chance. It might be said that your choice of subject becomes limited, but that need not be so. It depends very much on how you treat it.

You could decide to write about a man who spent his whole life slaughtering animals for his weekly pay packet, then in middle-years rebels against this never-ending carnage and decides to join the side of the pigs, the sheep and the cattle. If you presented him as an ex-member of the Lancashire Fusiliers, a present member of the British Legion, helping the St John's Ambulance Brigade for two nights a week and who also writes a letter to the Queen and tries to obstruct fox-hunting and badger-baiting, then it will be obvious that a great deal of your story would be quite outside the understanding and interest of potential foreign listeners, who do not have any of these British institutions. You could understand that there could be no great interest in your play abroad.

You may decide that you will write the same story, but leave out all of the British 'bits'. Make him the international man of conscience and use only those situations, organisations and people which exist in any country. But you still may be wasting your time.

You have used as your theme a rejection against the slaughter of animals for the table. For the British audience you should have no trouble in so slanting your treatment so that it appeals to the basic British attitude of being kind to animals.

It should not shock you to find that many citizens in other parts of the world are made of much stronger fibre, and would wonder what the devil all the fuss was about. We have to eat in order to live, don't we? So an international radio play has to be geared to the interest of the common man, and not to his particular culture and morals.

And the treatment of this particular story and theme must be of a kind which easily lends itself to local adaptation – your policeman becomes a gendarme – your Edinburgh station or district becomes Sydney or Milan. In this particular instance, your theme stands no broad international chance at all.

There is just one more aspect of this 'milking' principle, and that is milking the area in which you have some particular flair, success, understanding or some related ideas.

Let us say that you have written a very nice piece on the Victorian era. You have found that the dialogue of both upper-class and lower-class people just rolls out of your typewriter with no great effort. You have a feel for the period, and understand how those people would think and act, you understand how their social framework holds together. Now nobody is suggesting that from here on you write nothing but Victorian-type material. But you should be able to do so occasionally, shouldn't you? And you should be capable of going a few years earlier, or a few years later in order to get more of a range. And you should be able to get some TV treatments out of these radio scripts. And what about the stage plays and a novel or two?

We have made two quite opposing suggestions now.

One is that you should try your hand at anything and everything in order to discover what you do best – at the same time finding an area or two in which you can turn out a piece when you choose.

The second proposition is that you should find certain fixed stories and areas and milk them for all they are worth.

Bear them in mind until you have sold your first radio or TV script, then adapt them to whatever you feel is the right course for you.

The greatest delight any writer can enjoy is that of being free to write whatever he or she likes.

The greatest delight to be enjoyed from being a *selling* writer is that you really do understand precisely what the market likes to buy.

All art is involved with the communication of ideas and emotions. Successful Radio and TV writing is communicating at one and the same time with the greatest possible number. There's the delight, there's the satisfaction and there, too, are the material rewards – not to be sneezed at.

And that, as they say, is Q.E.D.